— PRAISE FOR —
"FROM WELFARE TO FARING WELL"

"As a young professional and burgeoning entrepreneur, Ken Brown's concept of "paid internships" changed how I view my past and present work experiences and will influence the assignments (a.k.a. "jobs") I choose in the future. His story proves that every young person needs a vision for their life and teaches us that every "job" is really a "paid internship" where we are to "learn everything we can, provide excellent service and move on when the time is right."

This book is an easy and enlightening read. I was going from page to page laughing and learning along the way. I would highly recommend this book for young people who need a little career advice or have ever considered owning their own business some day. Whether you're just graduating high school or college, or have been in the working world for a few years, you're sure to find encouragement, ideas and lessons you can use in this book. Taking a few hours to read this book will be a great investment in your future!

From Welfare to Faring Well is definitely a job well done!"

> — *Roland Hairston,* Founder,
> ChristCulture.com
> Editorial Assistant & Marketing
> Coordinator, Gospel Today magazine

"Wow! What a story of faith and commitment. Seldom does a book say it better or more powerfully than this one. **From Welfare to Faring Well** simplifies the principles for success and puts how we can overcome the most dire of circumstances and succeed in spite of the odds. Written in a language everyone can understand, I was motivated by Ken Brown's wisdom and insight. This book is a must read for all those who are serious about success and inspired by the word of God. Bravo to Ken for such a wonderful contribution to humankind."

> —*George C. Fraser,* Author,
> **Success Runs in Our Race**

"**From Welfare to Faring Well** is a quick read for long lasting inspiration. Ken Brown provides easy-to-grasp principles and biblical truths that are life changing. It changed his life - it will change yours!"

> — *Farrah Gray,* best selling Author of
> **Reallionaire: Nine Steps to Becoming
> Rich from the Inside Out**

"The title of Ken Brown's book tells us that it's a failure-to-success story. If that's all the book contained, it would be just another victorious testimony. This book is more: It's also about values, ethics, and faith. He openly shares the principle of success—and they work for anyone. "

> — *Cecil ("Cec") Murphey*, Writer,
> co-writer, ghostwriter of 100 books including-
> **Gifted Hands: The Ben Carson Story** and
> **Committed But Flawed**

"Ken's story of welfare to work reveals the passion of which dreams are made of. As one of seven siblings raised by a grandmother on welfare this story of survival in the midst of trials will help every reader understand that God is the author and finisher of our fate.

From Welfare to Faring Well will help every reader especially our youth understand the rewards and favor of spiritual values despite the many challenges one may face on the path of significance in life. I value Ken Brown's commitment to write this book as a testament of how every challenge you face in life equips you for God's purpose for your life. The law of association says you will become the top five people you associate with the most. Choose your associates wisely, apply these principles to your life and value the challenges you face as sacrifices for a greater purpose you will dominate on planet earth, our inheritance."

> — *Jerome Edmondson*, President
> Christian Business Network-Entrepreneur
> Training Institute; Senior Partner, Edmondson
> Associates; Minority Denny's Franchise Owner
> and Author of **Maximizing Misfortune**

"Ken Brown's story is more moving than a good Friday night drama, and that's because Jesus Christ Himself is Writer, Creator and Executive Producer. Only God can take our tears and turn them into tender mercies. **From Welfare to Faring Well** is a message of messed up stuff transformed into ministry. For those who feel trapped by circumstances, Ken Brown has a word for you: your life counts, if you live it for Christ. You can do good - and do well. Praise God!"

> — *Andria Hall*, Broadcast Journalist/former
> CNN Anchor/Author of **The Walk at Work:
> Seven Steps to Spiritual Success on
> the Job**, www.TheWalkatWork.com

"Ken Brown wrote a story that is very much aligned and powerful with 1 Kings 17 which should be entitled ' Your Place of Assignment.' Every step of Ken's journey, he was being led by the Holy Spirit to find his place of assignment. Great read!"

> — *Donald Snider*, President-CEO,
> Paper-Plas, Inc., President-CEO, Abbeville
> Treats, Inc. and Chairman of First Spirit
> Bancorp

"You'll never be the same after you read Ken Brown's testimony in **From Welfare to Faring Well**. His story will cause you to rise up and go after your victory in God. Based on the promises of God's Word and a servant-leader attitude, you'll see that you can rise above challenges just like Ken did. Ken shows how vision, faith and integrity of heart are key elements to success. You'll be inspired after reading this book to pursue your destiny and purpose."

> — *Ed Gray*, Author of
> **40 Days to a Life of G.O.L.D.** and
> national motivational speaker
> www.EdGraySpeaks.com

"Ken's story can't really be contained in a book. The inspiration just leaps off the page. You see the threads that held his life together and the favor that keeps promoting him. This is a book you'll want to read over and over - but you'd be in for a real treat when you hear him speak. So much energy and passion - you can't help be motivated after one of his speeches."

> — *Pamela Perry*, President,
> American Christian Writers/Detroit Chapter

"Clearly, **From Welfare to Faring Well**, shows the divine making of an entrepreneur. While Ken Brown was working for *Marriott International, Aramark, Wendy's International, Grandma Gebhardt's Cookies, AWG, Lorenzo's Bistro and McDonalds'*, he was actually working for himself as well. Each job was considered a paid internship. Each challenge created character and contacts. Each risk revealed rewards and relationships. His story can become your story."

> — *Angelo B. Henderson*, Pulitzer Prize Winner,
> Radio Talk Show Host and Associate Pastor,
> www.Angeloink.com

"Ken Brown is not just a story of rags to riches - it's about God's faithfulness. When you read Ken's story, you'll be inspired to know God more intimately because it is Him who gives us the power to get wealth. **From Welfare to Faring Well** is one of the most remarkable modern-day stories of faith you'd ever read."

> — *Rev. Rose Grant*, Author,
> **God's Way to Possessing Wealth,**
> **www.rosegrantministries.com**

FROM Welfare TO FARING WELL

KENNETH BROWN

WITH PATRICK BORDERS

— FOREWORD BY LES BROWN —

KEN BROWN MINISTRIES • SOUTHFIELD, MICHIGAN

All Scripture quotations are taken from
The Holy Bible, King James Version

ISBN 978-0-9768742-0-1

Published by:
Ken Brown Ministries
www.kenbrownministries.com

Printed and bound in the United States of America
By Sheridan Books, Chelsea, Michigan
Cover & Interior Design by LaTanya Orr-Terry, LTerry Design
Edited by Patrick Borders, Skyla P. Thomas

DEDICATION

This book is dedicated to my parents *John H. Brown Jr. and Regina Brown* who by example showed me to live beyond my circumstances with integrity and passion. They always provided me with hope for a better tomorrow, unshakable faith and unlimited possibilities. They showed me that the best way to predict your future is to create it. For that I dedicated not only this book but, my life to them.

To Granny Celeste Cheatem — who was always there to deposit those nuggets of wisdom, knowledge and understanding. She taught me that we live to give and Granny has always been a living example of love, faith and courage. Thank you for always, always being there. For this I dedicate this book and my life to you.

To my wife Deidre — According to the book of Proverbs-*whosoever findeth a wife findeth a good thing and obtainth favour with the Lord*. When we met 25 years ago in high school little did I know, I had found my good thing. You truly are a phenomenal wife, mother, and friend. I thank God for you and your unconditional love and support. You are the wind beneath my wings. For this I dedicate this book and my life to you.

To my Three sons — *Austin, Bradley, and Drake*. Gentlemen, being your father is my greatest reward. I love each of you in unique and unexplainable ways. It is my hope that this book and my life serves as an example that all of your dreams are possible. Remember God promised to bless us as far as our eyes could see. Dream big and remember that all things are possible through Christ who strengthens' you.

To my siblings — John H. Brown III, Gwendolyn, Regina and Lorretta — if I could have chosen my brother and sisters, I would have chosen you. We have weathered some fierce storms together. Through it all, we've stayed together. Thank you for your confidence, love and support. For this I dedicate this book and my life to you.

ACKNOWLEDGEMENTS

I t is my belief that people come into your life for a reason, a season or a life time. All of my life lessons have been experienced at different places and with a wide variety of people. Attempting to name everyone individually would be unfair. I may miss someone. I would instead like to thank God for gracing me with so many special people (you know who you are) Who have enriched my life. I will be forever grateful. However, I must mention my Dream Team. These people have made an indelible impression on me.

Stephan Franklin and Shawn Moore — You have always been true friends. I appreciate your brutal honesty, even when it hurt. Thank for keeping it real and holding me and yourselves to a higher standard. Thank you for helping me remember that a test of a man is the fight that makes.

Archie Tolar — Thank for seeing and nuturing the vision when no one else would stay the course. I will see you at the top.

Mark Burrell — Thank God for your gentle spirit. You were amazing friend until the end. Words can not express how much I miss and appreciate you. (Rest in Peace)

Uncle Sonny and Uncle Brother — Thank you for teaching to me to live with integrity. You both were living examples of love and commitment. I am standing on your shoulders.

Edie Waddell and Eric Waddell — Thank you for seeing and believing in my dream. Thank you for my Golden Opportunity.

Chuck Goldberg — Thank you for allowing me to think out of the box. You taught me how lead with excellence.

Charlie Robinson — I appreciate you allowing me pick your brain and shadow you to learn the business. Thank for the confidence.

Ruby Coats —Thank you for always being there for me. I have always admired you strength and courage. Thank you for allowing me to share my life with your only daughter.

Marc and Pam Perry — Thank you for guiding me through this entire process. Thank you for your tireless efforts and support. Ministry Marketing Solutions has been a blessing.

Patrick Borders — Thank you for getting the story out of me. You have an incredible gift. You did a masterful job of bringing my words to life — for that I will be forever grateful.

My McDonalds' family — The entire staff of our company — The Brown Food Group Inc.— Thank you for allowing me the pleasure serving you and serving with you everyday. I love and appreciate each and everyone of you. Thank you for carrying out the vision.

LaTanya Orr-Terry — Thank you for the outstanding graphic design. Your work is heads and shoulders above the rest. Thanks for operating with a spirit of excellence. The Lord set us up as classmates in high school for such a time as this.

FOREWORD

By Les Brown

As I scanned the room, waiting for the next speaker to present to my speaker development summit,– the air was filled with excitement, anxiety and fear; while all at the same time a young man stood up — when his name was called — head held high, and back erect as he reached for the microphone. Staring at the audience from behind his thick, rimmed glasses, he spoke with a passion that clearly indicated that he was a man on mission to change the world. You could hear a pin drop as Ken Brown, dedicated family man, entrepreneur, author, dynamic, powerful speaker and servant leader (as he desires to be known) told his compelling and inspiring story. He was born to teenaged parents, one of five children. His family — because of many hardships, was evicted numerous times. Ken shared with us, as he will with you in his first book, how he rose from poverty to power. Most importantly, how you can too– regardless of where you find yourself as it relates to your goals and dreams. Each page will encourage you to serve in excellence at all times, under all circumstances. This is Ken Brown's life-example. It has been said that people form habits and habits create futures. Ken believes your habits are a product of your thoughts which help to form your character and ultimately — will create an incredible future for you.

When Ken speaks to our youth, the church, community or business leaders, he drives home the thought, with deep conviction, that life is about choices. At a time when so many people are feeling fearful in the face of record high job layoffs, home foreclosures, bankruptcies, and jobs being sent overseas, Ken reminds us that it doesn't matter what happens to you, but how you choose to deal with it. He speaks from experience, given the adverse, poverty-stricken circumstances that he was born into. He made the choice, at an early age not to be a victim of his environment and end-up like so many of his playmates that he lived amongst on the south side of Chicago. In this life-changing book, he teaches us the step-by-step formula that will transform your life. It is a formula that he created. Ken believes when a person holds themselves 100 percent responsible and accountable for the results they want to achieve, life takes on a whole new meaning. I have watched, with admiration as he urges audiences to live with integrity, treat everyone with respect and hold themselves to a higher standard than the average person. In doing this, you will not have enough room to receive the blessings life has in store.

Ken Brown is truly a messenger of hope and a shining example that his methods work. I am honored to have him as a friend, business partner, a mentee as I share the stage across this country. In this book, Ken Brown is serving notice to the world that he is a force with which to be reckoned. Get ready for some great things to happen to you and through you, as you take in his life principles. After completing this book, your life will NEVER be the same.

INTRODUCTION

By Simon T. Bailey,
author of *Release Your Brilliance*

You are holding in your hands one of the most important books of this new millennium. I invite you to open your mind to revelatory truth that will give you a rocket boost into your destiny. You're not an accident or a mistake. The world is a better place because you're here. The leaves clap their hands at the sound of your voice. You have the power to gather the wind of energy in your fist and use your breath to blow it in the direction of your future. The sun rises to signify your ascension into the stratosphere of unlimited opportunity. This book will demystify the questions from your past, thus igniting a fresh perspective for the future.

Ken Brown is one of the most inspiring, insightful and fresh voices in the 21st century. His desire to be transparent, authentic and 100 percent for real will connect to the dream seed inside of your spirit. I am confident that your life will be tremendously impacted as you study your reflection in the mirror called **From Welfare to Faring Well**. This book was written for those who feel -- or have ever felt -- stuck on the treadmill of life. Every pressure-cooker job, disrespectful boss, surprising layoff and unexpected salary freeze that was meant to leave you trapped in the basement of limitation will instead become a sustaining force as you ascend the staircase of possibility.

As an avid reader and author, I am inspired by writers who share their naked truth as a way of humanizing their journey. All of us have a story. Some people hide behind their story. Some people change their story to make people like them and a few people have the courage share their pain. They give voice to the hidden struggles of the past. As they write they discover that their words become an instrument of healing for themselves and those who read the intent behind the content.

This book is a spiritual treasure that will connect to those who are doing well, living on top of the mountain of life but are spiritually impoverished. It will also connect to those who feel struck and are striving for more in their lives. In this book Ken shares timeless spiritual wisdom that will enable you to transform from the inside out. I am so glad that Mu'dear instilled in Ken's heart a love for the God of the Universe and creator of all good things. If he can do it for Ken Brown, what can he do for you? Where you've been in your past is the foundation for where you are going.

I am convinced that your life will never be the same after you read Ken's first of what I'm sure will be many bestselling books. As you read there will be times when think that he has lived with you or someone told him your personal business. The fact of the matter is that this book is a prophetic word sent to light your internal candle of unlimited possibility. Simon Says…to transition **From Welfare to Faring Well**.

TABLE OF CONTENTS

PART 3 — BUILT TO SERVE

PART 1 —
LESSONS OF
CHILDHOOD

chapter one

EVICTED

*"The gem cannot be polished without friction nor
the child of God cleansed without adversity."*
— Unknown

I stared at the old green cafeteria doors as my friends sat around me and ate their lunch. To my right sat my new best friend, Mark Burrell, and around the eight-foot table were six other boys—friends I'd made during that first year at the Willibrord Catholic High School in 1980. Through the windows of the doors, I watched the March wind blow through the inner city of Chicago.

Mark and the other boys were busy eating and laughing, but I couldn't take my eyes off those doors. I knew my family had failed to contact the sheriff's department that morning—the first morning in a month we hadn't called. The judge had granted us "five days to vacate the premises," but our name never appeared on the daily eviction list. *Maybe it won't happen.*

Then I spotted Jerome Faulkner. He flung open those cafeteria doors and raced inside. Our eyes met. *What's Jerome doing here?*

Jerome lived next door to me. He was one of eight

children in the Faulkner family, and although he'd graduated from high school, he still lived at home.

Then I realized why he'd come to my school. It had happened.

I wanted to hide from my friends—slink under the table and crawl away. My stomach churned. I knew life would never be the same again. I wanted to die.

"Ken," he shouted as he walked toward me. "Ken!"

I turned away and looked toward Mark. *Maybe Jerome didn't see me.*

But Mark heard Jerome's voice and watched him approach. The blood rushed to my face and it burned. I wanted to run, but my body wouldn't move.

Jerome stood in front of me. "Ken."

I couldn't ignore him. I stared at him.

"You gotta come home," he said. "Your stuff's in the street."

He smiled. Just a little bit, but he smiled, nonetheless.

"What are you talking about?"

"The sheriff evicted you. Everything's outside."

Mark and my other friends stopped eating. No one spoke. I felt their gazes.

"Oh, I know all about that. We're moving."

"Moving?" Jerome said. "Your stuff's in the street, and you're just moving?"

"Yeah. Didn't you know? We're moving to that house on the corner. Those Hispanic folks are leaving."

"Nah, man. You've been evicted. There's no truck. Everything's out—tables, beds, chairs. Everything. Just stacked. Haphazard-like." He smiled again, almost with a sneer, like he was enjoying the drama. I don't think he wanted to smile, he just couldn't help himself. "People are picking through it. You gotta come home."

I wiped my palms on my pants and felt the sweat bead on my forehead. I wanted to dry my forehead, but I didn't want my friends to notice, so I ignored it and stared at the table. "I tell ya, we're moving," I mumbled. "To the house on the other corner."

Jerome's smile disappeared, and he gazed back, looking confused.

I stood up, turned away, and walked off, leaving my lunch and Jerome behind. Before I reached the door, tears filled my eyes and blurred my sight.

"Kenny?" Mark called.

I shoved through the doors and raced down the hall, wiping the tears as I ran. "We're moving. We're moving." My penny loafers slapped the linoleum, and my tie flew over my right shoulder. I ran down the stairs, drying my eyes as I passed a teacher.

"You okay, Kenny?"

I didn't stop. At the bottom of the stairs, I pushed through the doors and darted toward the office. There, outside the office, stood my brother John and Mr. Weston— the assistant principal.

I slowed down and walked to them. I tried to slow my breathing.

John looked stoic. His lower jaw stuck out, and he stared at the blank cinderblock wall behind Mr. Weston.

Mr. Weston gazed down at me. His brow furrowed in a look of concern. "Your mom called me and told me what's going on. Everything's going to be okay."

It's out. They had evicted us. It was real.

A pressure rose inside of me, up through my chest,

and into my face. I cried into my hands. Cried hard. Tears flowed down my cheeks and over my hands. I cried like a baby, and I didn't care who saw me.

Mr. Weston wrapped his long arms around me and held me. I pressed my face against his red crewneck sweater, which covered his large belly. "If you need anything at all, please let me know." He patted my back. "Tell your mother, if you need anything at all, I might be able to help."

Mr. Weston was one of the sternest, yet kindest men I knew. He was a big white man, running a school that was almost entirely black. He strutted through the halls each day, holding a paddle and seeking out troublemakers. But he loved us. Everyone knew he loved us. We were his children.

After I settled down, I wiped my face with the cuff of my shirt. I gazed at the floor and stared at his black wing-tip shoes. I was glad he was there.

"Everything's going to be okay," he said again. "But I think you both should catch a bus home."

John and I dragged ourselves on the city bus and sat down—John next to a window and me next to him. We didn't talk. I glanced up at John. He stared out the window—his jaw jutted out and his eyes were hard and focused. He crossed his arms across his broad chest.

I turned toward the opposite window and listened to the monotonous hum of the bus. It was a beautiful March day; the sun shone bright and thawed the Chicago streets after a cold winter. I watched the homes pass by and felt disconnected from the rest of the world—a world full of people moving forward with their lives—happy and secure.

I shook my head. *It can't be. We have to be moving.*

But I knew life would never be the same. We'd lived on borrowed time.

"We're going to move like normal folks," my mother had said. "If we show up on the list before we move, we'll mobilize. You'll stay home from school, we'll pack our stuff and find a new place."

After thirty-five minutes, we got off on our street, South Bishop, and began the one-mile walk to our home. It felt like forever.

When I was six years old, gangs of white teenagers chased me down South Bishop as I walked to school. They never did catch me. But now I felt like I'd been beaten to a pulp. My legs trembled, and I could barely feel my feet as they stepped along the cracked sidewalk.

"We must be moving to the house down the street," I said to John. "Mu'dear said they're selling it, and we're going to rent it." We called our mother "Mu'dear," which is short for Mother Dear.

John glared straight ahead. He knew it wasn't true, and so did I.

We came within four blocks of our home, and our corner house came into view. I spotted the stack of belongings sitting out front—a blob of different colored objects. But as we walked, the blob grew, and I could identify the various mounds piled on the sidewalk and the side of the street. With each step, the stacks got bigger, and I saw my bunk bed, the glass coffee table, and a chair from the living room.

I ran the last block to our house.

Two large men carried my mother's dresser out of our front door and placed it on the sidewalk. A sheriff's deputy stood guard on our front porch. My father, who had moved out three years earlier, shifted stuff into a truck as fast as he could.

Mu'dear combed through piles, trying to find clothes. "Grab some clothes for a few days. Then help your dad get everything on the truck." She raced around the piles, sorting things and trying to protect stuff from breaking. She retrieved our baby pictures and diplomas and set them aside. Mu'dear was only four-foot-nine, but the moving men jumped out of her way whenever she crossed their path.

"I wasn't home when they started," she said. "People pilfered our things."

"Who?" I asked.

"Neighbors. Anyone who was around. They've taken our good glass lamps, our suede pictures, our porcelain statuettes, our end tables." She glared at some of our neighbors standing about thirty feet down the sidewalk. "Anything they could get their hands on."

People had rifled through the stacks and scattered unwanted items across the lawn. A painting of a panther lay at my feet with a rip down the middle—probably where someone had walked on it.

Stunned, I watched as Dad raced in and out of the truck. I felt disconnected from my body. Deep wrinkle lines stretched across Dad's forehead, and the muscles from his clenched jaw ran over his high cheekbones. He was strong and athletic, like John, and he carried as much as he could hold for each trip. Nothing was too heavy. But I saw that many of our possessions had already disappeared.

Dad stopped and glanced at me. "Hurry and help!"

I shoved my book bag in the car and combed through the piles of clothes, trying to find a few things. I grabbed what I needed. The two moving men brought out four black garbage bags of various belongings and dropped them by the other piles. The deputy closed the door and placed a huge padlock over the knob. He slapped a bright orange sticker on the door. It read: "No Trespassing. Violators will be Prosecuted."

Mu'dear scurried around and ignored the deputy.

I clenched the clothes in my hands. *That's my home! You can't take my home.* But he had. He'd kicked me out. Out of the house we had built for ourselves. The house I'd lived in most of my life. The house where we sold candy out of the basement window, where we played football on our large backyard, and where we played with the water hose on hot summer days. It was my house, and I couldn't even go inside.

Ever again.

The crowd around us seemed to grow like a mound of swarming ants. Mrs. Faulkner, Jerome's mother, watched us from her kitchen window. The heat rose again in my face. I wanted to slink away and die. We'd been role models in the neighborhood. The Browns were smart. Upwardly mobile. People of integrity. But now we were a circus show.

We camouflaged our problems for a long time, but now they'd thrown us out of our home in disgrace.

"Come on, Kenny," my mother said. "Get those clothes in the car."

I tossed my handful of clothes in the trunk and helped Dad and John with our remaining belongings. Dad closed the truck and drove to a storage facility.

Mu'dear, my four siblings, and I got in the car. I looked back at our house as we drove away—the tan siding and brown brick shrinking from my view. My friends would come home and discover us gone. No time for good-byes. It was better to avoid the embarrassment, anyway.

"God's got a plan for us yet," Mu'dear said. "The next

house will be bigger and better. Just you wait and see."

chapter two

CHILDREN
HAVING
CHILDREN

*"Train the child in the way he should go: and when
he is old, he will not depart from it."* — Proverbs 22:6

I was thirteen when we were evicted. It was a young age to deal with such trauma, but at least Mu'dear protected our dreams and my right to be a child. Mu'dear's childhood, on the other hand, ended when she was thirteen.

That's how old she was when she became a mother.

As I grew up, I became aware of the small age difference between my parents and me. We talked a lot in our family, and my constant curiosity led me to ask questions of my parents and grandparents:

"Mu'dear, my teacher thought you were my sister when she met you. Why do people think you're my sister?"

"Granny, why does Mr. Faulkner look so much older than Daddy? Mr. Faulkner has kids the same age as us."

Over time, my family revealed bits and pieces of information about my parents' first years together.

My father, John Brown Jr., played a lot of basketball

in his neighborhood—around 38ᵗʰ and Indiana on the south side of the inner city. A basketball friend of his, Tyrone, was also a friend with my mother, Regina Cheatem. Through Tyrone, my parents met in the summer of 1963 and became interested in each other. Dad had just completed the eighth grade, and Mu'dear had finished seventh.

Unfortunately for them, my grandmother, Celeste, forbid my mother from seeing John.

"You're too young to date," Granny said. "Besides, that John Brown plays sports too much. He'll never amount to anything."

But Granny's ban didn't deter my mother. Mu'dear was born with a strong will, and she didn't take no for an answer. She dated my father in secret.

One evening that summer, Granny invited some of her lady friends over to play cards. While the women laughed and carried on, my mother snuck my father through the back door and up the stairs. Eventually, they went into the bathroom and had sex in the bathtub. As it sometimes happens with teenagers, it only took one time to get pregnant.

Mu'dear hid her pregnancy the best she could. I don't know what she thought she'd do long-term; I don't think she knew. But fear prevented her from saying anything.

Her brother Sonny grew suspicious, though. He was twelve years older and wise to the world. "Mama, Regina's pregnant," he said a few months after my parents' encounter in the bathtub. "She's been throwing up, and her face is filling out."

"She can't be," Granny said. "It's impossible."

"I'm telling you, she is."

My Uncle Sonny persisted in his claim, so Granny decided to find out. She was a Creole from Louisiana and had her own methods for diagnosing various ailments. After Mu'dear denied being pregnant, Granny boiled her a cup of pepper tea; a drink, that according to a Creole wives' tale, a pregnant woman won't be able to keep down. Again drawing on her strong will, Mu'dear drank the cup and didn't bring it back up.

"See," Granny said to Sonny. "She's fine. No pregnancy."

But the morning sickness worsened, and Sonny noticed. Early one Sunday morning, he raced down the stairs. "Mama! Mama! Regina's upstairs in the washroom throwing up again. I told you she's pregnant."

Granny ran upstairs. After Mu'dear finished vomiting, Granny sat Mu'dear down on the toilet and started asking questions.

My mother cried and confessed that she'd had sex with my father. And, yes, she was probably pregnant.

"What have you done? You're only thirteen years old, and you've thrown your life away!"

Granny grabbed her by the wrist, and pulling her along, stormed down the stairs. "We're not going to church. Sit yourself down in the living room. We're going to have a meeting and figure out what to do."

She called my Dad's mother, Annie Mae Brown, told her what had happened, and asked her and my father to come over. She also called her ex-husband, my grandfather Walter Cheatem.

Later that morning, my two grandmothers, my grandfather, and my parents met in Granny's living room and discussed what to do.

"We make choices in life," Granny told my parents. "You made your choice. Now you'll deal with the consequences."

My grandfather John Sr., lived in Wildwood, Florida, and was not at the meeting. He owned a restaurant there, and at one time, the entire family—my grandfather, Grandma, my Aunt Jean, and Dad—worked in the place. But when Dad was thirteen, Grandma divorced my grandfather and moved to Chicago, taking along her two children. Soon after the move, Dad met Mom.

Grandma and her family still own land in Wildwood. At one time, she thought Disney might purchase the land to put through a highway, but it never happened.

After moving to Chicago, Grandma stayed in the food business—working various restaurant jobs and eventually landing a job with the Hyatt Corporation. When she retired many years later, Hyatt renamed the restaurant where she had worked, calling it Annie's Café.

My grandmother Cheatem was also from the South—born on a sharecropper's farm near New Orleans. The white owner of the farm had an affair with my great-grandmother, and Granny was the result—a fact that was kept secret from Granny for most of her life.

"I'll make sure Celeste is taken care of," the man promised her mother, "if you keep everything hush-hush."

Granny has a very fair complexion and beautiful straight hair. When she was a child, other children ostracized her because she was so different.

My grandmother and grandfather Cheatem met in Louisiana while he was in the military. When he got out, they moved to Chicago. But after having three children, they divorced, and Granny raised my mother and her two brothers on her own. My grandfather Cheatem eventually remarried and started another family, but he still remained an important figure in my mother's life.

During the meeting, Dad sat on Granny's ottoman and trembled. He put his hands under his thighs to hide the shaking, but his shoulders and jaw still quivered noticeably. I'm sure he feared my grandmother would, at any moment, throw him out the window.

Granny interrogated my parents. "How did this happen? Where were you? Why did you do it?"

Mu'dear told her the truth, except she didn't have a good answer for why she did it.

"Was this the first time?"

"Yes, Mama."

The rays from the morning sun beamed through the window and into the living room. The room was immaculate; not a speck of dust could be seen. My grandmother Brown sat quietly, not moving except to crack a slight smile at Mu'dear. The prospects of a baby in the family actually seemed to make Grandma happy. My grandfather bent forward and cupped his forehead in his hands. He shook his head back and forth. He served as a deacon in his church—Omega Missionary Baptist—and was mortified by the whole affair.

For what seemed like forever to Mu'dear, Granny rebuked her and Dad. Granny's eyes bulged as she fumed. "We're a wholesome family. We don't go around having sex at thirteen!" She sighed and shook her head. "I can't believe I let this happen. While I was at home, no less. Now, I've got another baby to rear."

Despite her dismay, she stuck to her pro-life beliefs.

Granny took a deep breath. "First things first. There'll be no abortion. I won't have abortions taking place in this family. Are we all agreed?"

My parents and my grandmother Brown nodded. My grandfather didn't need to answer. Everyone knew where he stood.

"Okay then. The baby will stay here. Regina will stay in school, and I'll raise the child."

"Celeste," my grandfather said. "I'd like to send Regina to Louisiana to have the baby. After it's born, she can return. We won't say anything for a while."

Understanding my grandfather's embarrassment, Granny agreed. She then looked at my father. "You should be ashamed of yourself, young man. You've messed up a lot of lives."

My father glanced up. He still shook. "I'm going to take responsibility, ma'am. I'm not going to disappear. I'm already working a paper route, and I'll get another job to make sure the baby's taken care of."

Within a few weeks after the meeting, Mu'dear dropped out of elementary school (our elementary schools back then went through eighth grade) and left for Louisiana. There, she lived with her grandmother Annie Freeman and gave birth to her first child, John Brown III. When Johnny was two months old, Mu'dear returned to Chicago with the baby.

Dad started the ninth grade at Englewood High School and visited my mother and brother whenever he could. Dad followed through on his promise. He worked his paper route before school, and he worked delivering milk in the afternoons. His milk route income went to buy Pampers and Gerber baby food.

Mu'dear's elementary school principal didn't want her

to return to school. "We don't want her being a bad influence to the other girls," the principal said.

Granny got my grandfather involved and they fought for my mother to get back in. The principal eventually relented, and she was able to graduate—although a year later than scheduled.

Dad wanted to play an active role in his child's life. Many boys in his situation would have treated their son as a toy, playing with him when it was convenient, but taking no responsibility for his care. Or worse, they would have abandoned the child. But in that sense at least, Dad showed maturity beyond his years.

At first, Granny didn't allow him too much responsibility. He'd proven himself irresponsible in having sex with Mu'dear, and he was still just a boy. Plus, Granny had committed herself to raising Johnny. She cared for him while Regina went to school. She sewed all his clothes, fed him, changed his diapers—just about everything. Granny and Johnny developed a special bond that endures to this day.

One thing changed after Mu'dear's return: Granny permitted my parents to continue their relationship. From that point on, my parents were a couple. They didn't run from their responsibilities. They committed themselves to Johnny and to each other. Everyone in the community knew it. Their friends knew it. And their parents knew it.

Mu'dear and Dad spent a lot of time together at Granny's house. So, it wasn't a total surprise, although a disappointment to Granny, when Mu'dear became pregnant again—sixteen months after Johnny's birth. I was born in September of 1966—Dad had just started eleventh grade and

Mu'dear ninth grade.

While he didn't necessarily take responsible action when it came to having sex with my mother, Dad continued to work hard and show maturity in other ways. He landed a job as a hotel restaurant cook. Though still in school, he made pretty good money. His mother worked a lot, and Dad had a strong independent streak, so he decided to move out of his home and rent an apartment. There, he could spend time with Mu'dear, Johnny, and me without anyone else around.

One night when I was a few months old, Dad asked if he could keep me at his place for the night. Granny consented.

Dad lived in a basement apartment, and apparently, the old cast iron radiator didn't work too well. The apartment was cold and drafty. A winter wind blew all night.

Early the next morning, my Grandma Brown showed up at Dad's door to check on me. "Where's Kenny?"

"He's sleeping on the bed."

Grandma says she ran over to the bed and discovered me stiff and blue—barely breathing. "Dear Lord, please save my baby!" Then she whapped me on the chest, and I wailed.

She picked me up, and within a few minutes, my skin turned pink and warmth returned to my body.

Two months later, Mu'dear was pregnant again. By this time, the family knew she and Dad would stay together. They asked their parents for permission to get married and everyone agreed. In the winter of 1967, more than three years after Johnny was born, Mu'dear, Dad, and my three grandparents drove to the Cook County Courthouse. There, my grandparents signed papers granting my parents the right to get married. A judge signed more papers and then proclaimed my parents as husband and wife. After that,

Mu'dear dropped out of school to care for her family, while Dad finished up high school and graduated on time.

It'd be easy to say that my parents made plenty of mistakes as teenagers. But I know God had a plan. Future years proved that. He brought Mu'dear and Dad together for a purpose, so I'm not sure I can really consider their actions mistakes.

At times they were irresponsible, and at other times they showed responsibility beyond their years. But they were kids. What was I doing at thirteen or fourteen? Despite the trials I endured, I lived relatively free of adult burdens.

In some ways, my parents died when Johnny was born—they lost a part of their youth to raise us. But as the years unfolded, they taught us to live a life of abundance, even when we were living a life of material scarcity.

Wisdom was growing in them.

chapter three

MOVING UP

"Problems are only opportunities in
work clothes." — Henry J. Kaiser

"Life is ten percent what happens to you,"
Dad often said, "and ninety percent how
you respond."

Dad worked hard. He wanted to learn new things
and tackle new challenges. When Dad took the milk delivery
job to help provide for Johnny, not only was he accepting
responsibility, but also I think he was responding to his desire
to better himself.

After he started at the restaurant, he earned a
promotion to egg cook and made enough money to afford a
larger apartment. We moved into a two-bedroom apartment
at 7405 Vincennes Avenue. It was on the first floor of an all-
brick building. It was small, but at the time we didn't need
much room.

Mom focused on taking care of Johnny and me, and
Dad got a second job at Ray Foley's Restaurant on the north
side of Chicago. For most of his years as a cook, Dad worked

two jobs. He left for work around five in the morning and didn't return home until the evening. But on the weekends, he still found energy to interact with John and me—he would wrestle with us on the floor, take us for walks, or play a game with us.

Both of my parents believed strongly in the education of their children. "Education is opportunity," they said. (As we got older, Mu'dear insisted that all her children would attend college—something nobody on either side of my family had done. "When you turn eighteen," she said, "you're going to college. You have to get out of my home and go to school. I won't let you stay here anymore.")

When I was ready for preschool, Mu'dear enrolled me in the Saint Peter and Paul Head Start Program. Head Start is a government-funded program that helps low-income children get ready for grade school.

The Saint Peter and Paul School was located around the corner from our apartment. Mu'dear walked me to school each day and met me after school to walk me home. Our neighborhood wasn't dangerous, but she was still concerned with my safety.

"Never get into anybody's car after school," she warned. "If I'm not there when you get out, then just wait. I'll be by within a few minutes."

But when it came time for Mu'dear to give birth to my sister Gwendolyn, she asked a friend to pick me up. Mu'dear didn't have time to tell me about the change in plans. When her friend arrived at my school, I refused to get in her car— even though I knew who she was. I kept hearing Mu'dear's voice, "Don't get in anyone's car. Don't get in anyone's car...." I walked home that day, crying, as Mu'dear's friend drove behind me.

Gwen was born a few days before Christmas, and about six months later, Mu'dear became pregnant again. A year after Gwen came along, Mu'dear gave birth to twins. But the babies were born too early and measured about the length of Daddy's hands. Their hearts hadn't fully developed. The twins died a few days later. Mu'dear and Daddy named them Mitchell and Michael and gave them a regular burial.

But my parents were young—still teenagers—and apparently quite fertile. It wasn't long after the twins died that Mu'dear became pregnant once again. With a growing family, Dad decided that we'd move into a house.

"They're building new homes on South Bishop Street, and we're going to buy one. They're trying to integrate the area. It's a great neighborhood, and the prices are good." Through his hard work, Dad saved up for a down payment. "It's time for the Browns to become homeowners."

Yeah! Johnny and I jumped up with excitement.

Since our lease was coming due on Vincennes Avenue, Dad and Mu'dear decided not to renew it. Instead, we moved in with my Grandma Brown while our house was being built. We lived with my grandmother for only six months, but it was six of the most difficult months I remember as a small child.

Grandma lived on one side of a small, two-bedroom duplex. It also had a small basement with a bedroom. My Aunt Jean had divorced her husband and was already living there with her three children. Aunt Jean slept in the basement bedroom with her daughter, and her two sons slept in the extra upstairs bedroom. Grandma had also recently married, so with her husband, Aunt Jean's family, and us, eleven people had to squeeze into that small home. An alcove sat off Grandma's living room, and in this area, Dad and Mu'dear set up their rollaway twin bed each night. John, Gwen, and I slept on the living room floor.

The tight quarters provoked a lot of tension between Mu'dear and Aunt Jean—and also between us Brown children and our cousins. I had to be careful not to touch anybody else's stuff. Grandma had her stuff, and Aunt Jean and her kids had their stuff, and I'd get fussed at if I went near any of it. I couldn't go in their rooms. And when we opened the refrigerator, we had to make sure we only ate the food that belonged to our part of the family.

My parents envisioned a better life for themselves and their kids, and I think this added to the animosity. At the time, Aunt Jean and Dad were heading in different directions. Aunt Jean was a recently divorced, working mother who'd fallen back on living at Grandma's to make ends meet. Dad, on the other hand, was happily married and provided for us financially while Mu'dear stayed home. We were moving up— we were building a home, Dad had started culinary school at the University of Chicago, and Johnny and I attended Head Start.

"Why are you staying home and putting the kids in Head Start?" Aunt Jean asked Mu'dear. "They should be home. Or you should be working."

Aunt Jean looked at our preschool as simply a daycare. She didn't understand my parent's vision for our education.

My cousins fed off their mother's bitterness. I wore a nice uniform to school each day, which annoyed Chucky. "Look at you in your fancy uniform. You think you're better than us," he said. "I'll be glad when you finally move out."

Too many people were living in one place. Everyone was on top of each other, and my family needed space to be together. Grandma was very gracious to let us stay with her, and she rarely complained. But I felt like an intruder and a burden.

Before we moved out, however, Grandma gave me a great example of her generous spirit. Grandma stored some of her food in the kitchen refrigerator, but she also kept a small refrigerator in her bedroom closet. In that refrigerator she kept things like juice, jelly, and peanut butter. She often returned home from work carrying grocery bags, and she'd make a beeline toward her room to stash away the food. Under no circumstances were we allowed to go into her room.

But before Christmas that year, Chucky decided to sneak into Grandma's closet when she wasn't home and raid her food supply. John and I tagged along.

We tiptoed into her room, hoping the wood floor wouldn't creak. As Chucky reach for the doorknob, I stared at us in the full-length mirror that covered the door. *We probably shouldn't be doing this.*

Chucky turned the knob, and the door groaned. Our mouths gaped open.

Instead of food, we were shocked to see Christmas gifts stacked high in the closet. Red wrapping paper, green ribbons, and gold bows reflected the afternoon light from Grandma's window. She had outdone herself. That was a great Christmas, and I'll never forget her generosity.

One Saturday morning, Dad shook my shoulder as I slept on the floor. "Everybody up! We're taking a ride."

We'd taken Saturday drives before while living with Grandma—mostly to catch a breather from our cramped quarters—but this ride was different. I gazed out the car window as we drove through the south side of Chicago—

from Grandma's at 95th Street to 122nd Street. At 122nd, we turned onto South Bishop Street. Dad slowed the car as we passed by bulldozers and neat stacks of lumber. Construction crews had recently leveled some of the lots, and on others, they'd poured the foundations.

This is our new neighborhood!

As we moved down the street, I spotted more homes with the framing completed. In my young mind, I'd never thought about how homes were constructed. In a way, I thought that my apartment and my grandparents' homes always existed. Now I understood how they were built from the ground up. *Cool!*

Daddy slowed down and came to a stop in front of a newly-framed house. It sat on a corner lot.

This is it! I can't believe we're gonna live here.

I glanced farther down the road and saw that railroad tracks crossed our street. Older homes sat on the other side, and I spotted boys riding their bikes in the street. The boys were Caucasian.

We hopped out of the car, and Dad gave us a tour of our new home. The interior walls weren't up yet, and as Dad spoke, Johnny and I jumped from room to room through the invisible walls.

"This is where the kitchen will be," Dad said. "And here's the living room."

The stairs and second level flooring were already in. We walked upstairs.

"And here's your room," he said to Johnny and me. "Your new bunk beds will go in the corner."

Bunk beds!

"Next week they'll start on the siding and the brick. Then they'll put up the walls. We'll have fresh sod, and we'll have bushes under all the lower windows."

Mu'dear smiled. "It'll be ready in two to three months. After we move in, Daddy will build a swing set in the back."

Our own swing set! I couldn't believe it. *We're going to live like kings.*

Every other week, we'd take a family drive to check on the progress of our home. I felt like I'd explode with anticipation as I counted down the days to our move. The Browns were getting their own house—with a large grassy lot for playing football and a quiet neighborhood for hanging out with friends. A place to grow up in the comforting presence of my parents and siblings.

"Today's moving day!" Mu'dear called. Johnny, Gwen, and I jumped up and threw our clothes on. We loaded up the car trunk with our belongings and headed off to South Bishop Street.

I never want to sleep on anyone's floor again.

My stomach fluttered, and I bounced up and down on the back seat; I could barely contain my excitement. After turning onto our road, I saw the house. The newly painted tan siding glistened from the morning sun. The brown bricks on the lower half of the house gave it the look of a solid foundation. The new sod cried out for a game of football.

As we pulled up to the house, I saw the black street numbers nailed over the door: 1-2-1-4-3. I ran up the walkway and waited—rocking from foot to foot—as Daddy opened the door. He swung it open, and I saw my grandmother Cheatem sitting on a brand new recliner.

A black and white tiger pattern covered the huge chair. Granny grinned at us. "Welcome home!"

Movers had delivered all new furniture and had placed it around the house. Daddy and Mu'dear saved their money while living with Grandma and used their savings to buy all new furnishings. There were new chairs, cocktail tables, and sofa tables. Under the sofa tables, Dad had set up red lights that flashed on the walls.

Awesome!

Black and white suede wallpaper covered the walls, and red shag carpeting covered the floors. It was very 1970s, but it was beautiful and it was ours.

Johnny and I ran upstairs and found our new oak bunk bed—the most exciting piece of furniture in the house. Coming back downstairs, I sauntered around and touched everything: the suede walls, the shag carpet, the smooth glass tabletops. Everything. I shut my eyes and took in the new house smells. It was almost too much to absorb. I got very little sleep that night.

In hindsight, the home was a bit small—especially compared to today's standards. But it was much bigger than our old apartment, and we didn't have to share it with our cousins. Plus, it was a full single-dwelling house. On a corner lot, no less.

"You can't be what you can't see," Mu'dear often said. My parents had a vision. And they turned their vision of a family home into a reality.

I thought we'd be in that house forever.

chapter four

EARLY YEARS ON SOUTH BISHOP STREET

"Regardless of circumstances each man lives in a world of his own making." — Joseph Murray Emms

As I walked to the Edward H. White Elementary School with my brother and new friends, I heard a car idling behind us. I glanced back. A blue Mustang pulled alongside us, and a white teenager rolled down the window. Three other white teenagers sat in the car.

"Hey, niggers! Where you going?"

At first I was confused. I didn't understand why they spoke to us like that, and I thought it was obvious where we were going. The guy scowled. My breathing quickened, and I felt the sudden urge to run. I turned away and ignored him. None of us responded.

"Niggers! Go home. We don't want you here!"

We walked faster. My heart pounded against my chest. Although, it was cold outside, beads of sweat dripped down my forehead.

The driver spit, hitting Darnell in the face, and that

triggered an even greater fear in us. We raced down the sidewalk as if we were running for our lives. The white boys hounded us the rest of the way to school—cursing and yelling "nigger" all the way there.

My school was brand-new and named after an astronaut who died in the Apollo 3 launch pad test four years earlier in 1967. The school was located in Calumet Park—the Caucasian area across the railroad tracks from our house. My first year, the school was seventy percent white and thirty percent black.

Mu'dear had recently given birth to my sister Regina and was pregnant again with her final child, Loretta, so she couldn't drive us to school. Within our first few weeks, Johnny and I made friends with our neighbors, Darnell and Maurice Faulkner, and together, we trekked the six blocks across the tracks and through Calumet Park.

The school had an open lunch, which meant I had to return home to eat each day. When we left for lunch on the day we were chased, the same boys were waiting and pursued us to our houses. And then back to school. And then home again.

Almost every day during first grade, various groups of white teenagers—usually in groups of four, and usually in a car—would chase and threaten us. I was overweight and not a good runner. I feared that one day I'd fall, and the white boys would catch me and kill me.

Our principal, Mr. Blanks, reminded the students to walk in groups. "Have unity. Don't leave anyone alone when you're walking to and from school."

One day during that first winter, school let out as usual and everyone exited the main entrance. Suddenly, a flurry of snowballs rained down on us. As I scurried back inside, I glanced behind and spotted the mob. At least fifty white boys stood outside the entrance and heaved snowballs, swung chains, or smacked sticks against the palm of their hands.

"Go home!" they chanted.

Mr. Blanks corralled us farther inside and called the police. They arrived within a few minutes and dispersed the crowd.

Those Caucasian people didn't just antagonize the children; they threatened people of all ages. Dad loved to play basketball, but all the sports fields and basketball courts were located in the white area of Calumet Park. One day he decided to play basketball at one of the courts.

"I'm not gonna let them tell us we can't play." He persuaded some friends to join him, and they headed across the tracks. "We'll be respectful. But we're gonna play."

About twenty minutes later, I looked out the window and saw Dad and his friends racing back across the tracks. He ran in his socks—he'd run so fast that his feet had flown out of his shoes. A second later, a car sped up to the tracks and screeched to a halt. Two white men jumped out, gathered some rocks from the railroad bed, and threw them at Dad and his friends. Fortunately, nobody was hurt. I was scared for Dad, but as time passed, the thought of Dad running out of his shoes struck me as funny, and I teased him about it.

Only African-American families had moved into our new neighborhood. Sometimes the sound of a brick crashing through a neighbor's window startled us awake in the middle of the night. That never happened to us; it only happened to homes where a black teenager lived. Those black kids attended Fenger High School, and their white classmates were the ones throwing the bricks.

I never witnessed any actual violence. It was always

threats of violence, and usually only the teenagers threatened us. But I'm sure their parents influenced them. Later, I realized the conflict didn't have as much to do with skin color, as it had to do with economics. The white people in the area were scared—scared of losing property values, losing their jobs, or simply of change.

Over the next several years, most of the white families abandoned the area. By the fourth grade, the proportion of white and black students had switched—now seventy percent of the students were African-American. By the time I graduated eighth grade, it was ninety percent.

I didn't hate Caucasians because of those experiences— I was too terrified to hate them. It would take several more years before I overcame my fear of white people.

Regardless of how other people acted, however, my parents insisted that I hold myself to high standards and be a person of integrity. My brother was my role model. I admired him, and whenever he did something, I wanted to tag along—even when he misbehaved.

One day, Johnny told me to follow him into my parent's room. "I got something cool to show you."

We snuck into their room, and I followed him up to the bed. They slept on a huge round bed that sat on a platform, and above the bed, my father had hung a red porcelain ashtray. They were still young—and foolish at times. Even as a seven-year-old, I understood the dangers of smoking in bed.

John walked to Mu'dear's nightstand and pulled out a black lighter. "Watch this."

He flicked the lighter. It sparked, and a small flame rose from the top.

"Whaddya doing?" I asked.

"Just watch. I'm gonna burn the ashtray, but it won't burn or melt." He held the flame under the ashtray for a minute or so.

I shuffled my feet back and forth. *We're gonna get caught or set the house on fire.*

John flicked off the lighter, grabbed the ashtray, and turned it over. A black spot, about an inch round, had materialized on the bottom. He grabbed a wet cloth and scrubbed off the sooty mark. It wiped right off.

"Hey," I said. "That's cool. How'd you do that?" John's trick fascinated me. "Let me do that."

"No. You're too young to use a lighter."

I pleaded with him, but he refused. He put the lighter in the nightstand and told me to leave with him.

But I didn't.

After John left, I grabbed the lighter and repeated the trick. Unfortunately, I held it too close and burned the ashtray. I threw the lighter in the drawer and ran out of the room—hoping no one would notice.

"Johnny! Kenny! Come here!"

We ran to my mother in the kitchen and stood at attention.

"Okay. Who did it? Who burned the ashtray?" Mu'dear may have been small, but she seemed like a giant when angry. Sweat beaded on her nose, and she jabbed her finger at our faces. "Who was playing with fire?"

She glared at me.

"Naw, I didn't do it." I said.

But Mu'dear could break us down when we lied or hid stuff from her. Johnny finally ratted me out. "Kenny did it. I was showing him how to do it, but I wiped it off. He went back and did it himself."

She glared at me. "Is that true?"

"No, Mu'dear. I didn't do it. I didn't do it."

She just stared at me. I started crying and confessed. I couldn't keep up my lie while facing her glare.

Pow! She smacked me in the mouth. Mu'dear had a backhand as strong as Serena Williams. If I told a lie, or didn't show respect, she'd smack in the mouth before I knew what hit me. Mu'dear shooed me to my bedroom and spanked me the whole way there.

I cried like a baby.

Later that evening, she sat me down at the kitchen table. "Why'd you lie?"

"I was scared I'd get a whippin'."

"Listen," she said, pointing that accusing finger at me, "I don't care how scared you are. You don't lie. Ever. If you lie, you'll steal. And if you steal, you'll kill." She lowered her voice to a calmer tone. "In life, Kenny, people may get angry when you tell the truth, but you still need to do it. You have to have integrity."

Mu'dear kept me up late talking—repeating the importance of having integrity and an honorable reputation. She also lectured me on the dangers of fire. "You don't mess with fire. You could have burned the house down. Understand?"

"Yes," I said. But I kept thinking, *You shouldn't keep an ashtray in your room. Smoking in bed is dangerous.*

The next morning I peeked in my parents' room as I was headed downstairs. The ashtray was gone. I never saw it again.

Mu'dear and Dad disciplined me, but they were also open to learning lessons themselves. They didn't see themselves as perfect, and they weren't too proud to adjust their habits. I think they understood that we also discerned right from wrong by watching them. "The eyes and ears are the windows to one's soul," Mu'dear often said.

Mu'dear was tough on the outside but kind on the inside. She used that swift backhand on us whenever she felt the need. If I said something rude, then—bam—I'd feel the sting on my mouth and start to cry. But she always sat me down and talked about it. "Do you understand why I popped you?"

We talked for hours. "You must have high standards. You must treat people as you'd like to be treated. You must be honest with them." By the time the evening was over, we'd laugh about whatever had started the whole thing.

We talked a lot in our household. Mu'dear and Dad loved to talk, and they didn't keep much from us. They'd tell us things about their childhood, their first years together, and losing the twins.

At night, we'd pop popcorn and gather around the television to watch *Creature Feature*, *Good Times*, or *Hawaii Five-O*. Or we'd play games like *Monopoly* or *Got a Minute*. With *Got a Minute*, we used a word cube to make up as many words as we could within one minute. Often, we argued over some of the less-conventional words we came up with, but it was in good fun.

Throughout it all, we talked—during the games, the television shows, or any other time. We often visited our grandparents on Christmas and other special occasions. There, we talked some more. I might play with my cousins for an hour, but after that, I sat and joined the adult conversations or simply listened. I was a sponge, soaking up their stories and opinions.

My parents encouraged my curiosity and indulged me by answering almost any question I asked. I'm sure they recognized I was a receptive audience, and that I wanted to learn from them. Dad, in particular, took many opportunities to teach me about the world.

chapter five

LESSONS FROM DADDY

"He that getteth wisdom loveth his own soul; he that keepeth understanding shall find good." — Proverbs 19:8

"Johnny, Kenny," Dad said, "time to get up. I'm gonna take you to work today." Even though it was a summer morning, and I liked sleeping in, I jumped out of bed and high-fived Johnny. "All right!"

Dad still worked two jobs. He'd worked his way through the cooking ranks—starting out as an egg cook, then fire cook, and then broiler cook. Now, after earning his degree in culinary arts from the University of Chicago, he was a certified chef.

Although he worked a lot, he still paid attention to his children. He talked with us in the morning, and he made sure to eat breakfast with us each day. Mu'dear made him eggs, bacon, toast, and coffee. Right before he left, Johnny and I would run to the door and give him a kiss, and then we'd race back to the table. Dad liked his eggs over-easy, and he often left one egg, as well as pieces of bacon and toast for us to fight over. We tried to bump each other out of the way as we sopped up his remaining yoke with the toast.

But on this summer morning, Dad wasn't leaving us behind to fight over his food. He was taking us with him.

As Dad drove us to the Hyatt, I fidgeted with excitement. The working world was a big mystery to me. At the hotel, Dad got out of the car, smoothed out his black pants, put on his pressed white jacket, and donned his tall white hat. He looked in the mirror and smiled.

We walked behind the restaurant and entered through a back door. As Dad opened the door, a symphony of controlled chaos greeted me: bacon sizzled on frying pans, plates clanged as they were slapped on metal tables, the dishwasher hummed and clinked, and people shouted: "Table two up," "I need my eggs," "Hot stuff coming through."

I don't think I'd seen so much busyness in my life. I stood frozen for a moment, taking in the activity.

Dad escorted us through the kitchen, giving us a tour as though we were hotel executives. He pointed out everything, like the deep fryer, convection oven, griddle, deck ovens, and walk-in freezer. He made sure we understood how everything worked and the responsibility of the person at each station.

As we walked past one of the stoves, a man turned around and smiled at us. "Whaddya got here, Buddy?"

Most people called my father Buddy—even my mother. It was an appropriate name, because he befriended almost everyone he met. He was the life of any party—he told great stories and jokes, and he loved to laugh.

Dad turned to the man and stood tall. "This is John the Third, and this is Kenny." He often made a big deal about John being the Third, which annoyed me.

Everywhere we walked in the kitchen, cooks turned

around and shook our hands. Then the waitresses came back to greet us and some even pinched our cheeks. Everyone wanted to meet John Brown's children.

I loved meeting Dad's friends, but something about the energy of that place also captured my attention. Cooking was in my blood: my grandfather owned a restaurant in Florida, Grandma Brown and Dad worked in restaurants, and Granny Cheatem and Mu'dear were incredible cooks. I couldn't stop staring at everything and everyone. The restaurant business bug had bitten me.

Whenever Dad started a job at a new restaurant, he took us for a tour. And the energy of each operation always excited me.

Dad tried to live by the words he preached. He walked the talk. And he talked a lot.

He lectured us on the importance of being independent thinkers and getting a good education. He talked to us during any activity—meals, watching television, or driving around the neighborhood.

"The masses are the asses," he said over dinner. "Sometimes, people are like sheep. They don't think for themselves. They'll go along with the group if they think it'll get them comfort or convenience."

He'd ask about school and our recent assignments. If John got an A on a test, Dad used him as an example for the rest of us. "Look at Johnny. He studies hard, and he's going places. The rest of you need to be like him."

Well, I'm trying, too! If Dad didn't praise me, then it made me feel bad about myself and mad at him for ignoring my efforts. But I have to admit, he also lit a fire in me to do better.

He even challenged Regina and Loretta, who were in preschool at a Head Start program. "Girls, count in Spanish," he'd command with a smile.

Regina and Loretta received Spanish lessons at school. "Uno. Dos. Tres. Cuatro…" they said.

"Excellent," Dad said, clapping.

When I talked, he made sure I spoke well. I might've been telling a story about something that happened that day, and I'd say something like: "I told Terrance I didn't want to do dat—"

Dad would interrupt. "Dat? What does dat mean?" He would lower his voice. "When you talk, Kenny, you need to talk with articulation. Pronounce your words. Be clear."

Even when we watched television, he found moments to teach us something. One evening while we watched Hawaii Five-O, he pointed at the television, identifying a character who didn't have a job and hung around with bad people.

"See him?" Dad said. "He's a lumpkin." Lumpkin was Dad's favorite term for a person who wasn't going anywhere—wasn't moving forward in life—just a lump on the earth. "You must make sure you find your purpose in life and live it. Don't be a lumpkin. Get educated. Read books. And don't do anything to hurt the Brown name."

Dad thought our name was a big deal, like we were the Kennedys or something. I knew better than to tarnish our family reputation.

On weekends, Dad took us wherever he was going, like to the store or to visit friends. Even driving around, he found moments to preach. He liked to make his lessons visual; he never missed an opportunity to point to a physical example, like he had with the character on Hawaii Five-O.

The McNeil Crane Company was a business located at the end of our street. They owned a large yard where trucks came in to load or unload their large cranes. Sometimes, Darnell Faulkner and I, along with other friends, played at the loading docks. We usually played a game called Strike Out—a take-off on baseball where we'd throw a rubber ball against a large X marked on the brick wall. Many people who hung out at the docks weren't boys, however, but grown men shooting dice or pitching pennies. They wasted hours and hours gambling and just hanging out.

Driving by McNeil, Dad pointed to the men. "See those guys? They're lumpkins. Someday they'll end up living on 79th Street, begging for whiskey from the liquor stores and leaving their children to run with the gangs."

He often used 79th Street as an example of where we'd end up if we didn't work hard and stick to our purpose. "Some of those men may've had tough lives. But life is ten percent what happens to you and ninety percent how you respond."

Later, while driving, he might discuss setting a good example for others. "How you behave affects, not just you, but other people." He pointed to the home of a family we knew. "Take Mr. Walker. I've heard him yelling at his sons for drinking alcohol. But then he throws these all-night parties, and you see people leaving drunk and driving home. He has no integrity with his kids. And they'll grow up to be lumpkins like their father."

The Jacksons were another family that set plenty of bad examples. They lived down the street, and both Mr. and Mrs. Jackson worked at a motor company plant. But it was well known that Mr. Jackson also did the numbers with fellow employees—meaning he was a loan shark.

The Jacksons made lots of money and spent all of it.

They owned a beautiful blue Cadillac and other high-end cars, wore the latest fashions, and dressed their house up with elaborate landscaping and fencing. They also hosted plenty of parties.

People came to our house to play football on our large yard or talk with my parents, but people came to the Jacksons for the parties. They charged a quarter to get in, and they'd let kids in, too. Throughout the house, people drank beer and liquor and listened to loud music. In the basement, guests did more nefarious things, like drugs.

I believe Mr. Jackson saw himself as a role model—financially and materially. He liked to prance around the neighborhood in his fancy clothes and show off his new cars.

Each Christmas, they showered their kids with presents. One year, they bought them a new pool table. Darnell and I were friends with one of their younger sons, Shawn, and the day after Christmas, he invited us over to play pool.

When Darnell and I walked inside the house, a strong odor like dirty gym socks hit us. Dust covered much of the furniture and a heavy layer of dirt ran along the baseboard. Only a few lights worked, casting a gray pall inside the house. Mr. and Mrs. Jackson had made a good show of prosperity from the outside, but the inside of their home seemed rotten.

In the kitchen, their daughter cooked a huge pot of chili. She had a little son who wandered out of the kitchen. He wore a brownish diaper and no shirt, and he sucked on a pacifier. "Hey, loser!" his mother yelled to him. "Get back here!"

Shawn said that his family had called the boy that because "he does everything wrong."

The boy stumbled past me and ignored his mother.

Both of Shawn's parents were at work, so the kids had the run of the house, as usual. We played pool for several hours that day and every day for about a week after Christmas. I never saw Shawn's parents during that time.

Around three o'clock each day, Shawn ate from the same supply of chili that his sister had made. While we shot pool, we also played a verbal game called the Dozens. In it, we tried to rag on each other—each time trying to top the insulting statement made before.

"Your mama's so fat," Darnell said to one of the other boys we played with, "when she gets on the scale, it says, 'To be continued.'"

When I didn't notice it was my turn to shoot pool, Shawn said, "You're so poor, you can't even pay attention."

"Well, you're so poor," I replied, "you can't afford to eat nothing but chili."

At the end of the week, however, Dad banned me from going to the Jackson's home. "You're spending too much time over there. The Jacksons make bad choices, and I don't want them influencing you."

I didn't fully understand it at the time, but later I saw Dad's point. He wanted me to have an upward vision—one that improved myself and my place in life.

But Mr. and Mrs. Jackson didn't seem to care about their kids; they just cared about money and the things money could buy. Their daughter eventually left home and moved in with her boyfriend. He abused her, and one night she called one of Shawn's older brothers and asked him to come get her. At her apartment, her brother and the boyfriend got into a fight, and the boyfriend shot and killed her brother.

The Jackson family went downhill after that. Gangs

were becoming popular in the area, and all the boys got involved in gang violence and selling drugs. Years later, when the little boy was twelve, he joined one of the largest gangs in Chicago. Even though he was young, he was ruthless and rose into the upper echelons of the gang, becoming a major leader before he was killed. Even Shawn eventually was killed in gang-related violence.

Dad understood what we were up against. "You become like the people you hang out with," he said. "Don't have a ghetto mentality." He knew how important it was to have a vision for our lives and to stick to that purpose. There were too many temptations in the inner city that could suck you down if you didn't stay focused.

Dad also had a vision for himself. He wanted to learn new things and make a positive impact on his community.

As he climbed the chef ranks, and conquered new challenges, cooking didn't fulfill his ambitions the way it once had. He grew bored and restless, like a soldier without a battle to fight.

His vision shifted away from cooking to other areas.

And that shift was about to change my family forever.

chapter six

Good-bye Daddy

"Go settetth the solitary in families: he bringeth out
those which are bound with chains: but the rebellious
dwell in a dry land." — Psalm 68:6

Dad's jobs were hectic, and they required a lot of physical labor. In the past, his passion for the work gave him the energy he needed. But now the strenuous work wore him out.

He came home each evening, gave us a kiss, and headed downstairs to his den—a place we called Daddy's Room. When he kissed me, he smelled of onions and sweat, and he clenched his jaw, like he was angry. He trudged down the stairs, walked into his room, and closed the door behind him.

Mu'dear understood his need for time alone. "Don't bother Daddy right now. He's tired and needs time to rest."

Immediately after he closed the door, he cranked up his large sound system—maybe playing Kool and the Gang or Aretha Franklin—and turned on his black lights. He'd decorated the room with a disco theme—covering his walls in psychedelic wallpaper and wild posters that seemed to come to life when the black lights illuminated them. One poster contained a black cobra with glowing green eyes.

Dad would sit on his leather recliner, light up a Winston, and relax. An hour later, Mu'dear would call us to dinner, and Dad would saunter upstairs—somewhat refreshed, but still not the vibrant person he was at breakfast.

One morning in 1975, when I was nine, Aunt Jean called Dad and asked him to take her and my cousins to Sears and Roebuck. Her kids needed clothes for the new school year, but Aunt Jean didn't own a car. Dad helped her whenever he could. My cousin Chucky even lived with us for a year when he was going through a tough period.

That morning while Aunt Jean and her kids shopped, Dad sat in the Sears parking lot and listened to Motown music on the radio. As he waited, a man walked beside Dad's car and knocked on the window. He wore a blue suit with a large political campaign button pinned on the lapel. Dad rolled down the window, and the man introduced himself. "I'm with the Independent Party, and I'm running for alderman."

The man talked about his campaign and his party's platform. Before he left, he gave Dad a flyer that would change his life.

The flyer talked about the Independent Party. The party based its platform on the need to change the world and "make it a better place for our children." The flyer stated that society needed to recapture the genius of classic philosophers like Plato and classical musicians like Beethoven. It painted a vision for the future that encouraged self-betterment and hope.

While he sat in the car, Dad studied the leaflet. And it triggered something in his soul.

Later, he called the phone number on the flyer and

asked to join the group. Before long, men from the organization picked him up for evening meetings in downtown Chicago. He attended their meetings only once a week at first. But after a few months, the frequency grew to twice a week, and finally, he seemed to go every other day.

He returned home from those meetings more energized than I'd seen in a long time. "Knowledge is currency," he said. And for him it was even more. It was food.

The people at the meetings fed him knowledge—knowledge about the world and literature and prospects for the future. He'd witnessed so much hopelessness in the inner city, and he wanted to lift up people.

Dad changed. He quit smoking. He read literature. And he took his new insights and shared them with other people. He spoke at churches and handed out party newspapers at the airport.

"I'm empowering people through knowledge. I'm helping them change the world."

He campaigned for Independent Party politicians, and at one point, ran for alderman himself. As he campaigned at various churches, I tagged along to run the overhead projector while he talked. He had always loved engaging in conversations, and that skill helped him become a great orator. In those churches, I observed the people's faces—the wide eyes and rapt attention.

These people really respect him.

He lost that campaign, but because he performed so well in public, and showed such passion for the cause, Dad rose through party ranks. The party promoted him to their steering committee.

At home, the topics of dinner conversation broadened to more than family or local issues. "The economy is global," he said. "Politics are global. You can't get locked up in just local events."

Most of the time when Dad spoke about those things, I just stared glassy-eyed at him. *What's he talking about?*

But he still tried to explain the concept of the global economy and talked about the Rockefellers, DuPonts, and Kennedys. He knew their entire family histories, and how they achieved their wealth and power. Jimmy Carter was running for president, and he knew all about him and his platform.

"The world isn't just circular; it's linear. Society builds upon itself," he said, his voice rising. "We're exploring the depths of space, and we're discovering new cures for diseases. You have to educate yourself and participate in the progress of mankind."

One time after I came home from school, Mu'dear told me some of Dad's friends would be joining us after dinner. I assumed it would be Dad's regular friends—the ones he played basketball with. But after we ate, Mu'dear started getting out cookies, chips, and drinks.

She doesn't get all this out for Dad's ball buddies.

The doorbell rang, and Dad opened the door. In walked a group of men—all of them Caucasian.

My pulse quickened, and I stepped back. I gaped as I watched them enter.

They wore black wingtip shoes, gray or tan trench coats, and ties. A couple of them wore argyle sweaters.

Dad introduced them. They politely greeted each of us and shook our hands.

After they took a seat in the family room, I leaned over to John and whispered, "What are they doing here?"

He shrugged his shoulders.

These are the people who didn't want us here. They're the

same type of people who threatened us.

I studied them from around the corner as they began their meeting. They ate our cookies and chips, drank from our cups, and talked about campaign strategy—where they'd deploy and what information they'd distribute.

Dad's eyes were attentive, and his shoulders leaned forward into the conversation. The faint hint of a smile traced his lips.

I went to bed before the meeting finished. In the morning, I started down the stairs and stopped midway— shocked to see one of the men asleep on our couch. One of our blankets covered him, and one of his white feet stuck out from underneath. I stared at him as if he was from Mars.

I continued down the stairs and the floor creaked. The man awoke.

"Good morning, Kenny." He smiled. "It was a late meeting, and I live a long way from here, so your dad let me crash on the sofa."

He was very friendly as we talked that morning. For the first time, my fear of Caucasians faded.

As Dad changed, he also altered his favorite hangout— his den. Only now, it provided less an escape from the world, and became more a library to the world. Out went Kool and the Gang and in came Beethoven and Bach. Out went the posters and the black lights. And in came a large cherry desk and office chair.

To me, the desk symbolized the dramatic change in my father. It represented the greater vision he had for himself. It was his prized possession; he didn't allow anyone to place food, drink, or anything else on it.

From his desk, he wrote his speeches and read the works of Socrates, Plato, Aristotle, Shakespeare, and his favorite—Augustine. He read three newspapers: the Detroit Free Press, New York Times, and Los Angeles Times. After reading the papers, he gathered his children around. "You have to have a global mentality. Let me tell you what's going on in the world."

I didn't understand half of what he said, but he captivated me by his confidence and passion. *He's the smartest man in the world.*

In one year's time, he became a new creature. Like it says in the Bible, you can't pour new wine into old wineskins, or the old wineskins will burst. As such, Dad's old wineskin— his old life—began to crack.

His committee work energized him, but he came home from his cooking job each day even more dejected and frustrated. "I feel like a slave to my job. I don't know how much longer I can do that type of work."

Dad's side of my family saw his self-improvement and thought it was a good thing. But Mu'dear's family considered it an unhealthy obsession.

My curiosity got the best of me many times, and I eavesdropped on conversations between members of my family.

"Buddy's losing his mind," I heard Granny tell my mother once. "He's joined a cult."

"He's gone crazy," my Uncle Sonny said. "People are starting to talk."

As Dad dedicated himself further to the committee, he cut back on his chef work. The committee provided him a $200 per week salary, but it didn't come close to the lost restaurant income. To make up for it, Mu'dear took a job at Michael Reese Hospital. She didn't want to, but she felt she had no choice.

One night after I went to bed, I heard my parents arguing. As soon as I heard their tense voices, I couldn't fall asleep. So instead, I sat at the top of the stairs and listened.

"You're spending a lot of time with the committee," Mu'dear said. "Too much time."

"You know this is my calling. I've found my purpose in life."

"What're you talking about? Your purpose is to provide for your family. To take care of your children."

"I am taking care of my children. It doesn't matter what we do in this house if we can't leave them a good world to live in. Our kids are the reason I'm trying to change things, trying to impact lives."

They continued the same argument, off and on, for months.

What's going on with them? We'd always been a happy family, and I didn't like some of the changes. I had a harder time sleeping at night—even after my parents went to bed.

Then one night, their argument seemed more intense. "I can't work at a restaurant no more," Dad said. "I can't do that type of work."

"What? You can't quit your job. You've got two sons, and I won't let them see you not working."

"What do you mean by not working, woman? I'm working as hard as any man. I'm working to make sure our kids have a better world to grow up in."

"The committee's not a job. Your chef work is a job."

"I can't do that no more. I'm not going to be a slave any longer."

There was a long silence. Then Mu'dear spoke in a

voice I could barely hear. "Well, you can't live in my house if you're not going to work a real job."

After they stopped arguing, I lay in bed with my knees bent up to my chest, and my body shook. I didn't fall asleep for several more hours.

The next day, Friday afternoon, I walked home after school. I was in fourth grade now at White Elementary. I crossed the tracks, leaving behind the Calumet Park neighborhood where white teenagers used to chase us and call us "nigger."

As I approached my block, I spotted an orange truck parked outside my house. A moment later, two white men—men from the committee—walked out our front door. They carried Dad's big cherry desk and loaded it onto the truck. Behind them, Dad carried a cardboard box.

What's going on? I stopped and let the truth slowly sink in. *No, it can't be!* I shook my head hard.

The desk represented Dad's vision for the future, and he was taking his vision somewhere else. I'd seen the warning signs—more and more time away from his home and more frequent arguments, but I still couldn't believe it.

I ran toward our house and straight to my father. "What's going on, Daddy?"

Dad furrowed his eyebrows. "You mean your mom didn't talk to you?"

"No. What do you mean?" My eyes started stinging, but I tried hard not to cry.

"Why don't you talk to me? I'm here. You've always told me what was going on."

He looked toward the street. "She didn't talk to you, huh?"

The reality of Dad leaving hit me like a two-by-four to the stomach. *This is real. I can't believe this is real.* "Wow," was all I could say.

I followed his gaze to the street. Mu'dear sat in a car with her lifelong friend, Claudette. They worked together at the hospital, and Claudette had brought Mu'dear home from work.

I stormed over to my mother. They were eating Church's fried chicken and laughed as they watched Dad load his belongings. The sight of them laughing angered me. I clenched my fists and felt the urge to punch the car as I approached it. "Mu'dear, what's going on?"

"I'll talk to you later."

"I want to know what's happening!"

"Daddy's leaving."

"How can you sit there and laugh and let him go?"

"I said we'd talk later. Now go inside."

"Fine!"

I couldn't hold back the tears any longer. I raced inside, stomped up the stairs, and collapsed on my bed. I slammed my face into my pillow, and it muffled my screams. "No! No!" I pounded my fists against the mattress, and I cried so hard, that the muscles in my stomach hurt.

How dare they not talk to me! We never had a family meeting about this. Never had nothing.

I'd been proud of our family. We laughed, talked, and played together. Mu'dear had stayed home with us. Dad worked hard, but he also had fun with us. He played football in the yard with us, and he played bongos on the porch for my friends when they came over.

The Browns were the role models for the community. Not people like the Jacksons. *Now we're over. Dad and Mu'dear have messed everything up!*

I dreaded tomorrow and having to show my face in the neighborhood.

I dreaded tomorrow and waking up without my father around.

chapter seven

MAKING LEMONADE FROM LEMONS

*"The bamboo which bends is stronger than
the oak which resist."* — Japanese

S oon after Dad left, Mu'dear's friend Claudette moved in with us—along with her four children. She'd recently left her husband and needed a place to stay. There was stuff everywhere. We had to share bedrooms, and her two oldest kids—Charlie and Tanya—fought almost non-stop. It reminded me of the chaotic conditions when we'd lived at Grandma Brown's. Only this time, we were the ones invaded.

Mu'dear and Claudette stayed up late each night and talked—about their man troubles and how bad men were in general. It seemed like they talked constantly.

I was ten years old and still craved the attention of my parents. *Mu'dear chased Dad away. And now she's let her friend come in and take all her time.* I hated it when Mu'dear talked to her about Daddy. It wasn't any of Claudette's business.

After Claudette went to bed one night, I stormed downstairs to confront Mu'dear. "It's your fault!" I screamed. "You ran Daddy off!"

Smack! That hand of hers flew to my mouth, and the sting around my lips triggered tears. She glared at me for a minute or so as I bawled. Then her face softened, and she wrapped her arms around me. "It's not like you won't see him," she said. "He's still going to come over. Every Sunday."

For six months, I tried to come to terms with my parents' divorce, but I couldn't get my thoughts straight with all the people in my home. And I was rarely up late enough to talk to Mu'dear without Claudette around. Finally, Claudette and her children moved out, and we had some time together as a family. Many nights, Mu'dear, John, and I stayed up late, talking and crying.

"We're going to make lemonade out of lemons," Mu'dear said.

The amount of crying she did surprised me. *She's hurting, too.* Now, I understood that all those hours she spent talking with Claudette helped her heal. *I just wish she'd talked to me, instead.*

Even without Claudette in the house, Mu'dear was far from finished talking to her friends and family. In fact, phone conversations became her obsession. She talked morning, noon, and night. After having breakfast with us, she'd call Claudette. When I came home for lunch, she'd be on the phone with her friend Dorothy. In the afternoon, it'd be Granny, and at night it'd be someone else.

I had easily listened in on Mu'dear's conversations with Claudette when she was living with us. But Mu'dear talked softer on the phone, and I couldn't hear her from the top of the stairs. One night, I crept downstairs after Mu'dear got on the phone. She stood at the sink washing dishes, and I snuck under the kitchen table, which was covered by a tablecloth. The sound of my heart pounded in my ears as I sat with my arms around my knees and prayed she wouldn't catch me. I sat so close to her that I could hear the person on the other end.

It was Granny. "John abandoned you," Granny said. "He let you down."

Surprisingly, Mu'dear defended him. "Nah. He would have stayed if I'd let him quit his job."

Other nights, I continued to listen in on Mu'dear's conversations from underneath the kitchen table. Sometimes, she'd even sit at the table—drinking coffee and smoking Winstons. But she was so wrapped up in her conversation that she never knew I was there.

All the talking seemed to help her. She came to terms with the divorce. Today, Mu'dear and Dad have a very good relationship. In fact, even back then, Mu'dear never badmouthed Dad in front of us.

After a while, I noticed more of her conversations revolved around other people's problems. Claudette, Dorothy, and others unloaded all their troubles on her.

"Hang tough," Mu'dear would say. And then I'd hear those familiar phrases: "Just watch. You'll make lemonade out of lemons." And one of Dad's favorites, "Life is ten percent what happens to you, and ninety percent how you respond."

I didn't understand how people could dump their problems on Mu'dear when she was going through so much. *How can you talk about your problems, lady? We've got enough of our own!*

People also came over and visited Mu'dear. Many of them were men, such as Mr. Faulkner, Mr. Calvin, and the man who'd introduced Mu'dear and Dad, Uncle Tyrone (even though we weren't related, we still called him uncle). They, too, unloaded their problems with life and relationships. Mu'dear listened and didn't judge, and they always seemed to feel better when they left.

But again I didn't understand. When I saw them smile and hug Mu'dear as they left, my muscles tightened. *You're just trying to steal my mother.* I thought every man had eyes for Mu'dear, and in my mind, she still belonged to Dad.

When Dad first moved out, he didn't live too far away. He stopped by every Sunday and spent the day with us. Usually by Saturday night, I couldn't wait to see him. But he'd show up on Sunday, and all the confusion and pain would return. *How could you leave me? Why didn't you talk to me before you left?* Then he'd leave Sunday night, and I'd start missing him all over again.

Our parents' divorce also angered Johnny, and sometimes, he didn't want to hang out with Dad. But I craved Dad's company. Every boy needs a father around—someone to show him how to be a man—and I guess I knew that instinctively. But I also had unresolved feelings with the way he left, and I sought his attention in order to gain some closure.

Even though Dad divorced my mother, he didn't divorce his children. He was a strong presence—still engaged in our lives and preaching his philosophy of improvement.

One evening, I stubbornly avoided my homework.

Mu'dear got frustrated. "I'm calling your father."

Oh, no. I'm in for it now.

Dad fussed at me over the phone. "What're you doing, giving your mother a hard time? Do your homework."

"Yes, sir."

"If you don't, I'll be over there in five minutes."

Many more times Mu'dear called, or threatened to call Dad when we misbehaved—especially when it came to school work.

They both still harped on the need for a good education. Before Dad left, my parents enrolled John in a Catholic private school for the fall. "You're still going to that Catholic school," Mu'dear told Johnny.

Eventually, Dad moved to the north side of Chicago, near Wrigley Field. He'd pick us up on Saturday afternoon, and we'd stay with him until Sunday evening. Sometimes, John or my sisters wouldn't go, but I always did.

By leaving home and visiting him, Dad exposed me to things I'd never experienced before. He took me to different types of restaurants or cooked different kinds of food at his apartment. He introduced me to variations of Jewish food, like lox and bagels, as well as spicy Ethiopian dishes, and Japanese sushi. Sometimes, he took me to the committee's offices in downtown Chicago, and I'd listen as they discussed campaign strategies.

We never watched television at Dad's apartment. Instead, he played classical music on the phonograph and gave us each a book to read. When our time was up, he made us report on the sections of the book we read.

If I resisted having to read, he'd give me his usual response. "What? Do you want to become a lumpkin—pitching pennies on Bishop or bumming around 79th Street?"

"No, sir," I'd say and open up my book.

When I graduated from elementary school, Dad arranged for me to attend a classical music camp in Pennsylvania. "You're older and need to get serious. It's time to stop listening to that rock music and broaden your horizons."

I spent four weeks in the woods, trying to learn how to play the violin. I can't say I really enjoyed myself—I never did learn to play the violin well. But I soaked up the newness of the experience. Dad helped me peek over the fence to see beyond my own backyard.

Over time, I appreciated some of the benefits from my parents' separation. I learned so many new things and enjoyed quality time with my father. On some days, Dad's departure still angered me. But on other days, I'd forget my bitterness and anxiously anticipate the next day I could spend with him.

With Dad giving up his chef work, our family finances deteriorated. Mu'dear tried different jobs. She worked at the hospital for a while, and then at Dunkin' Donuts and other places. But her jobs never lasted long.

She came home from work frustrated. Her evening attitude was similar to Dad's before he became involved with the committee. "Leave me alone," she'd snap if I tried to talk with her. But then she'd regret her tone and give me a hug. "I'm sorry. I'm having a tough time right now."

She didn't possess any skills outside the home. "My real job is being a mother." Sometimes, one of us got sick and that'd get in the way of working. Or she'd need to attend a school function, help us with our homework, or simply console us after a bad day at school. She didn't drive, and some of her jobs required her to take a long bus ride to the other side of town. She loved her family and couldn't stand being away from us.

Dad sent his small stipend each month, but that

didn't go far. Mu'dear was resourceful, though. She cooked and sold dinners to other families. And she sold snacks to neighborhood kids through the window in our basement. We'd go to the convenience store on State Street and load up on Snickers Bars, Mary Jane's, and various chips. Then we'd sell them for fifty-five cents. In the summertime, we also sold snow cones.

But it wasn't enough. I wasn't aware of our situation, but we were losing ground financially—building debts with the mortgage and utility companies. Things broke around the house—the washer and the television—and we couldn't afford to repair them. The lawn, which Dad had maintained and kept beautiful with flowers, gave way to weeds.

While we ate dinner one night, the light over the table flickered and then went off. It didn't come back on. The power in our entire house had shut off. I glanced out the window to the Faulkner's home; the light from their living room shone through the curtains.

"The electric company cut us off," Mu'dear said. "I haven't made payments for three months."

We sat in the dark, and I picked at my food. *What's gonna happen to us?*

That night, we moved to Granny's and stayed there for a week until Mu'dear scrounged up enough money to satisfy the electric company. We returned home, and a few months later, the gas company cut us off.

"Never mind the gas," Mu'dear said. "We'll use the electric skillet to cook with."

After the gas company reconnected us, the power went back off. This time we stayed home. For a few hours each evening, we ran an extension cord over to the Faulkner's, which powered a lamp so we could do our homework.

During that time, I occasionally heard Mu'dear weeping in her room. I peeked in one night and found her in bed, crying and reading her Bible.

I got back in bed and prayed. "God, please make things the way they were before. Please." More than anything in the world, I wanted to go to sleep and wake up in the morning to find my parents married and making enough money to pay the bills.

During the daytime, Mu'dear looked stressed—she clenched her jaw, and she'd stare hard out the window. Keeping up with our bills must've made her feel like one of those performers who spins plates on the end of sticks. Hopping from one plate to the other, he spins them, hoping they don't all come crashing down. Mu'dear kept up the balancing act as along as she could, but then the electric, gas, and telephone companies cut off our service at the same time.

"You need to go live with Granny for a while," she told us. "I'll stay here."

"You can't stay by yourself without power and gas," I said.

"I'll be fine. I need to be here."

When we walked out the door to catch the bus to Granny's, I turned back and glanced at Mu'dear. She smiled, but that didn't make me feel better. *I shouldn't be leaving. How's she going to handle this?*

For two weeks, Mu'dear lived by herself. In the dark. Without means to cook food or heat our house. Each day, I pictured her hungry and cold and sitting on her bed, crying.

When the utilities came on, and we returned home, Mu'dear appeared different. She seemed more at peace; the set of her mouth had relaxed, and she no longer glared out the window. "Things are going to be okay," she said.

After that, we started attending Grandpa's church—Omega Missionary Baptist—and Mu'dear talked more about God. "The Lord will take care of us." Something—or someone—had changed her during her two weeks in the darkness.

As I prepared to graduate from elementary school, Mu'dear reiterated her commitment to my education. "You're gonna go to the same school that Johnny's going to."

She's crazy. Johnny's school cost $100 a month per student. "How can two of us go to private school if we can't pay our bills."

But gangs had infiltrated our local public school—Fenger High. "I'll have no part of my children going to Fenger," Mu'dear said, her eyes set with determination.

In June 1980, I graduated from White Elementary School. My family, including Dad, sat in the front row and beamed with pride as I received my diploma. After that, I prepared to enter the Willibrord Catholic High School.

For the next four years, that school would be the most stable place in my life.

chapter eight

Poor in Money, Rich in Spirit

"Hope is that which makes us live today as if
tomorrow were yesterday." — Unknown

Toward the end of September 1979, Mu'dear
abandoned the idea of working a job and
applied for public assistance. I don't think
she considered it a defeat as much as she thought it was best
for her family. Now, she could be a mother again.

When our first welfare coupon arrived, Mu'dear took
us on the bus to the Currency Exchange on 119th and Halsted
Streets. At the exchange, we joined a long line of people
waiting to get their money and food stamps. A sea of opened
brown envelopes littered the floor around us.

After an hour, we arrived at the window. Mu'dear
pulled out her public assistance card and presented it to the
government worker. Her card displayed her picture, gave her
personal information, and with a big "5," told how many
dependents she had. The woman behind the window reached
into the cabinet behind her, gathered the appropriate amount
of cash and food stamps, placed them in a brown envelope,

and handed it to Mu'dear.

Once out of the line, Mu'dear showed us the money and stamps. "Welfare won't be a way of life," she said. "It's only a bridge to something bigger and better."

On the way home, we stopped at Belscott's Department Store to buy some badly needed clothes and shoes. Then Mu'dear treated us to lunch at McDonald's. I chewed my hamburger slowly and ate my French fries one at time—trying to savor the taste and enjoy the moment.

Maybe going to McDonald's wasn't the most financially prudent thing to do, but even during our most desperate times, Mu'dear tried to give us glimpses of normalcy. Every month after going to the Currency Exchange, we'd stop for a treat on the way home. Sometimes it was McDonald's, but other times Mu'dear took us to a place called the Millionaire's Club.

The Millionaire's Club was a fancy restaurant where the servers wore tuxedos and classical music played in the background. We didn't order anything much—maybe a snack and a drink. But Mu'dear exposed us to the Millionaire's Club for the same reason Dad sent me to the classical music camp: she wanted to keep our sights on a better way of life. "Someday you'll be able to eat here whenever you want and order whatever you want," Mu'dear said while we ate.

The importance of having hope grew as our financial condition crumbled. We continued riding the utilities merry-go-round as we lost, regained, and then lost again our electric, gas, and phone services. And sometimes, I heard Mu'dear on the phone, trying to negotiate a payment schedule for the payments we failed to make.

Food was also a struggle. We didn't starve, but we didn't eat well either. Gone were the days of steaks and pork chops. Now, we ate a lot of cereal, because cereal filled us up. Mu'dear bought the variety cereal packs, so we wouldn't get bored eating the same thing. My siblings and I fought over the Cap'n Crunch, Fruit Loops, Apple Jacks, and Frosted Flakes, but by the end of the month, we were forced to stomach the Special K and Product 19. We also ate government cheese, which came in large, hard blocks, and we drank government milk, which looked white, but tasted more like water.

One day, Mu'dear told us she couldn't afford to make our lunch for school any longer; we'd have to eat the free lunch the school provided. I'll never forget the next day—trudging up to the special area in the cafeteria that offered the free lunches. I felt as if all the eyes in the cafeteria followed me, and my face burned with embarrassment.

The free lunches came in a brown paper bag. We called the sandwiches "chokes" because the cafeteria kept them very cold, and they contained large blocks of cheese and no condiments.

I sat down and removed the choke from my bag, while I avoided looking at my friends around me. I bit into the sandwich and tried to chew it. It was cold and heavy in my mouth and hard to swallow. I only ate half of my choke that day.

"Can you please make our lunches again?" I asked Mu'dear a week later.

I must have made her feel guilty, because she agreed.

After that, Mu'dear would send me to Mario's Grocery, a little neighborhood store across the railroad tracks. I'd ask Mario for a loaf of Wonder Bread, half a pound of very thinly sliced bologna, and half a pound of very thinly sliced cheese. Mario was kind and smiled a lot. He even let us buy our food on credit. The sandwiches Mu'dear made didn't fill me, but

I didn't care. *At least I don't have to eat a free lunch in front of my friends.*

Somehow, Mu'dear scrounged up enough money to keep one creditor at bay before having to turn her attention to another. She refused to beg for money, but family members and close friends knew of our plight. Money seemed to show up just when we needed it.

During this time, Mu'dear's young faith grew stronger. She stayed up late into the night, praying, crying, and reading the Word. One night, I stopped in her room and found her sitting on the bed—tears rolling down her face. I sat next to her and wrapped my arm around her. "You okay?"

"Oh, don't worry," she said and smiled. "I'm crying out of joy. I feel the Lord's presence with us."

During the daytime, she played tapes of sermons from Omega Church and listened to gospel music. Mu'dear and Dad once had filled our home with the sounds of Motown and disco. But Dad had switched to the likes of Beethoven, and now Mu'dear completely switched to the likes of gospel singer Mahalia Jackson. The change was good, because in the months to come, Mu'dear needed every bit of her faith.

One afternoon, I arrived home from school and found Mu'dear sitting at the kitchen table. She held a letter in her hands, and her fingers trembled. "The mortgage company wants us out," she said.

I stood behind her and read the letter. It said: "We declare you in a state of default on your loan. As such, we find it necessary to foreclose on your property at 12143 South

Bishop Street. You have thirty days to vacate the premises."

These aren't premises. This is my home. They can't come along and take it away.

But Mu'dear explained how a mortgage worked, and that Tenniga-Bergstrom could, indeed, take away our home. I slumped onto a chair and stared at the table. It didn't seem possible. *They're stealing our home!*

Despite the notice, we didn't do anything different over the next several weeks. Mu'dear posted the letter on our refrigerator, so it wasn't like we ignored our impending eviction. We just didn't prepare to move. My siblings and I attended school like normal. Mu'dear stayed home and took care of the house. And prayed.

"Just have faith," she said. "God has a plan for us. Everything'll work out."

As the deadline approached, we took the bus to the LaSalle Street Courthouse to beg for an extension. I shook nervously as we approached the tall brown brick building and walked through the heavy wood doors. Long lines of people waited to funnel through the security station as a dozen Cook County officers directed the crowds and scanned them with metal detectors. As we walked up the stairs, our footsteps echoed off the high ceilings.

In the courtroom, I stared at the judge, a middle-aged Caucasian gentleman with salt-and-pepper hair. He wore a black robe and sat behind an enormous oak bench.

I listened to the parade of lenders and homeowners being processed before the judge.

A lender spoke, "Your Honor, Mr. Campbell has not made a payment in five months. I ask that you reject any further delays and allow us to proceed with foreclosure."

The homeowner spoke, "I just started a new job, and

I need just a little more time."

Back and forth they went.

The judge found in favor of the lender, and then bam, he slammed down his gavel.

Two more people stepped before the judge, pleaded their cases, and the judge rendered another judgment. Bam! Again went the gavel.

I studied the judge's decisions, trying to determine which way he might decide our case. And I tried not to jump whenever the gavel slammed.

Finally, it was Mu'dear's turn. She walked in front of the judge; her four-foot-nine frame seemed to shrink before the high bench. She stood erect and proud, though. "I have five children to take care of, Your Honor. And I don't have anywhere else to go."

"Mrs. Brown, you need to work on finding somewhere else to live. I'll give you a thirty-day extension." Bam went the gavel.

We took the bus home, somewhat relieved. "Things'll work out," Mu'dear said.

But as the next deadline approached, we still didn't have another place to live. That suited me just fine. I lived in the only home I wanted—the only neighborhood I wanted—and I clung to my hope we could stay there. Mu'dear had faith in God. And I had faith in her.

Mu'dear headed back down to the courthouse and finagled another thirty-day extension. But we still didn't move. She told us about a rental house down the street that a Hispanic family was supposed to be vacating, but they ended up staying. Granny didn't have room for us. And neither did Uncle Sonny or my other uncle, whom we called Uncle Brother.

I believe Mu'dear thought God would provide for us, but I also think she simply didn't know what to do. People thought she was crazy.

One day, we visited a friend of hers in the local housing project. "We'll only go for a short visit," she told us. "It's not safe enough to stay too long."

While we were there, Mu'dear's friend scolded her. "Girl, you're being stubborn. You need to move here. Rent is only $25 a month." Her friend looked at us kids. "And get those kids out of private school. Just who do you think you are?"

Later Mu'dear told me, "Don't worry. I'd never subject you kids to the projects. And I refuse to take you out of Willibrord."

Mu'dear even tithed ten percent of her welfare check to our church. Maybe she didn't handle money like other people, but whatever she did, she hoped her decisions were best in the eyes of God, and best for her children. "If we do the right things, God will provide."

At the end of the second thirty-day period, we made another trip to the courthouse. Again, I listened to the cases and tried to read the leniency or strictness of the judge.

A deep voice announced, "Mrs. Regina Brown. Foreclosure."

Mu'dear strode to the bench. "Your Honor, I'm still looking for another place to live."

"Ma'am, I've already granted you two extensions. I've been very lenient."

"But I have some money now that I can pay to the mortgage company."

"It's too late. They don't want your money now. They just want the premises."

"Sir, just thirty more days. That's all I need."

"I'm sorry, ma'am. You'll have to vacate the premises. The vacate order will be placed in five days."

Bam!

The echo of the gavel seemed to sound forever.

I sat in my seat with my mouth hanging open.

Mu'dear turned around—head held high—and walked back to us.

"What's that mean?" I asked her as we walked to the bus stop.

"It means we're out of time. We have to move."

"But where?"

"I don't know. I won't be a burden on nobody."

"The judge could've done something! That's not fair. He could've helped us."

I clenched my fists and pictured myself running back inside the courthouse and pummeling that judge. Years later, I realized that he had helped us, and he'd given us plenty of time. But back then, I thought he had turned a blind eye to the people who were stealing our home. I felt like the judge slammed that gavel right on my head.

Mu'dear learned she could call the sheriff's office each day and inquire about that day's eviction list. Each morning, we got up and called the office. The first few mornings, Mu'dear called. But after that, I made most of the calls. I was anxious to know if that day was *the day*.

"This is the Brown family. 12143 South Bishop. Are we on the vacate list for today?"

Call after call, the answer was no.

"God took care of it," Mu'dear responded after each one.

Our situation continued to fall apart, though. The

power company shut off our lights again. Mario reluctantly cut off our credit at his grocery store. We ate butter and sugar sandwiches.

Granny encouraged Mu'dear to take action and move. "What're you waiting for? God isn't going to move you. You gotta move yourself. You know you can live with me."

Granny lived in a one-bedroom apartment, and Mu'dear didn't want us sleeping on anybody's floor.

For two weeks, we didn't show up on the vacate list. More and more, Mu'dear believed it wouldn't happen. *Maybe she's right.*

Then the day came when we got too comfortable. We didn't make the phone call to the sheriff's office. That was the day Jerome Faulkner barged through those cafeteria doors and announced that all our possessions were sitting in the street.

chapter nine

SLEEPING ON FLOORS

"When the going get's tough, the tough get going."
— Robert Schuller

 As we drove to Uncle Brother's apartment, I leaned my head against the window and stared blankly ahead. I was frozen, as if the force of our eviction pressed down on me and kept me from moving, or for that matter, from making sense of my thoughts. My bag of clothes rested by my feet; Dad had taken our other stuff to storage.

I closed my eyes—more than anything, I wanted to go to sleep—and just get away from our situation.

We pulled up to Uncle Brother's apartment at 26th and Cermak Streets—a neighborhood dramatically different than ours at South Bishop. Hispanic people mostly populated the area, which in itself wasn't bad, just very different. The area was only a few blocks from a prison. Parked cars crammed both sides of the lane, and an overflowing trashcan littered the sidewalk. There were no trees, no manicured lawns, nowhere to play football—nowhere to play outside at all.

Uncle Brother's real name was Walter Cheatem—but everybody called him Brother. During the early 70s, he worked at a nearby steel mill. It was a good job and paid well. He drove a red Thunderbird convertible, and when I was younger, he used to stop by our house and give John and me rides. He drove real fast and loved life.

But the steel mill closed down. And Uncle Brother's spirit seemed to close down with it. He lost the car. And he started drinking.

Uncle Brother was the type of person I call a *camper*. As I grew up, I noticed that when people faced trouble in their lives, they responded in three different ways. The *quitters* gave up. The *campers* didn't quite give up, but their lives stopped moving forward. They figured they'd taken their one shot in life, and they'd lost it, and they just weren't going to try any longer. The *climbers* were the ones who kept bouncing back. They didn't accept the setbacks life dealt them; instead, they aspired to climb to something better.

Mu'dear was a *climber*. She may have used unorthodox methods at times, but she had a vision for the future, which she never stopped pursuing. Uncle Brother, on the other hand, stopped trying to improve his lot in life. He didn't roll over and die; he just assumed his life would never be as good as it was during the steel mill days, and he gave up hope.

He didn't turn bitter, though. He worked various odd jobs, and often worked with his brother Sonny—both of them were excellent carpenters and very handy. He was a generous man and well liked in his community. He helped out the older folks—doing repairs, moving stuff, or even creating artwork for them.

And like Mu'dear, he always welcomed friends into his home. The only difference with Mu'dear was that she and her friends didn't drink.

We stepped down the cracked concrete stairs and entered Uncle Brother's basement apartment. "Come on in. Come on in," he said. "Make yourself at home. Whatever you need, just let me know."

I dropped my bag of clothes in a corner of the living area. Uncle Brother offered each of us a seat at the kitchen table, and he poured some water. My siblings and I had sat in silence as we traveled to Uncle Brother's place, but now our worries caught up with us.

John, Gwen, and I bombarded Mu'dear with questions.

"How long are we staying here?" Johnny asked.

"What school will we go to?" I asked.

"When can we get the rest of our stuff?"

"What are we gonna do about school tomorrow?"

On and on we fired questions at her.

Mu'dear fingered her water glass. "I don't know. I don't know. Why are you asking me all this?" She covered her face with her hands and sobbed. "I don't know."

I stared out the kitchen window. The windows in Uncle Brother's apartment were high on the wall and looked out low on the sidewalk. I watched as people walked back and forth; only their feet and lower legs were visible. *I want to be one of those people and walk home.*

When night came, Uncle Brother retrieved some blankets and improvised beds for us on the floor. As I tried to sleep, his friends kept stopping by—they sauntered right in without knocking. They hung out in the kitchen, drank Mad Dog 20/20, and talked. They tried to be quiet and not bother us, but drunken people have a hard time talking softly.

The visitors stayed until three in the morning. Every twenty minutes or so, one of them stepped over me on their way to the bathroom. As they passed by, the sweet odor of liquor permeated the air and momentarily masked the mildew smell of the linoleum floor. Unable to sleep, I listened to their slurred conversations and the sounds of the neighborhood—feet pacing the sidewalk, cars honking, and the occasional ambulance siren blaring.

Tears rolled past my ear and onto the cold floor. *I just wanna sleep in my bed. In my home.*

I should've been grateful that Uncle Brother took us in. But the next morning when Mu'dear announced we were moving to Granny's, I felt relieved.

"Granny's will be closer to school," Mu'dear said. "We'll stay there for a few days."

"So we're still going to Willibrord?" I asked.

"Of course. Regardless of what happens, you're all going to college." She pointed a finger at me. "You have to get good schooling now so you'll be ready."

We moved over to Granny's house after breakfast. I felt like a hobo as I carried my one bag of clothes. Granny lived in a two-bedroom house that she rented on 117th and Halsted Streets. It was only a few blocks from school, which was on 113th. Granny's house provided a little more comfort. I still slept on the floor, but no rush of visitors stopped by to talk and drink.

Over the next few days, we stopped at the storage unit to retrieve some belongings. But one day, we pulled up to the storage unit and discovered a large padlock on the door.

"What's that for?" I asked.

Mu'dear knew exactly what it was for. She sighed. "I

haven't made the payments lately. They're taking our stuff."

When Dad had moved our belongings, he obtained a large storage unit—it needed to hold a houseful of stuff. But Mu'dear couldn't keep up the payments. The storage company foreclosed on our belongings, just like the mortgage company had foreclosed on our house. They auctioned off everything: furniture, remaining clothes, and even baby pictures.

Can things get any worse?

Despite struggling with the loss of our possessions, living at Granny's wasn't too bad. Just like we'd done at home, most of the time we hung around the kitchen table and talked. Or we gathered together in front of the television and watched our favorite shows. We talked about everything we'd gone through, and we even acted out plays about our experiences. Sometimes we cried. Other times we laughed. But Mu'dear encouraged us. "God's got something bigger and better in store for us," was her frequent refrain.

When I returned to Willibrord, I perpetuated the myth that my family had moved on our own accord. Only the assistant principal Mr. Weston and my friend Mark Burrell knew the truth.

"What happened the other day?" Mark asked, referring to the day Jerome came to tell me of our eviction. Mark squinched his face in a look of concern. "Did you get thrown out of your house like that guy said?"

I couldn't lie to Mark; he was too nice and supportive. "Yes," I mumbled. "We got evicted."

Mark was a bit overweight. He puffed out his large cheeks, and then let out a gust of air. The severity of my situation seemed to weigh heavily on him. "Everything'll work out, Ken Brown." He always called me by my full name. "Let me know if I can help."

Around everyone else, however, I acted like nothing had happened. I still wore the dress shirt and tie Dad had given me for school—so I didn't look poor. And I joked and played with my friends. But it wasn't long before people caught on that I was struggling with financial problems. If they hadn't already seen me getting my chokes in the cafeteria, they'd soon see me scrubbing toilets.

After the storage company took our belongings, Mu'dear told me to ask Mr. Weston if there was anything I could do to supplement my tuition payments. "See if you can help out with jobs around the school."

Later that day, I asked Mr. Weston. Earlier, he'd offered to help, so I wasn't nervous in approaching him.

"Sure," he said. "You can help Mr. Christianson, the custodian. We'll create a position for you. You'll be his assistant."

As it turned out, I worked for Mr. Christianson over the next three years, including during the summer and winter breaks. The school paid me twice a month—one check I gave to Mu'dear for living expenses, and the other covered my tuition. When I graduated four years later, we didn't owe the school any money.

Mr. Christianson was a short Irishman with a strong Irish brogue. After school, most of the staff doubled as a coach or club leader—Mr. Christianson coached the soccer team.

On my first day as the assistant custodian, I waited until most of the students left before reporting to Mr. Christianson.

Maybe I can do this job without anyone seeing me.

Mr. Christianson showed me how to operate the

big buffer to polish the hallway floors. I tried to operate the machine without it running away, while at the same time, looking over my shoulder to see if anyone spotted me. After I completed the hallway, I raced to quickly clean the men's and women's bathrooms before the CTA bus arrived to take me home. I finished by cleaning the tampon box in the last restroom. When I was done, I stuck my head out the bathroom door, and seeing no one in the hall, I darted out and to the bus stop.

Later that night I asked Mu'dear, "The other kids don't have to work, do I really have to? It's embarrassing."

Mu'dear set her jaw. "No. You don't have to work. You can go to Carver. Is that what you want?"

Carver High School was the closest public school to us now. It bordered a neighborhood called the Altgeld Gardens— a drug-infested housing project. Gangs had invaded Carver, and in fact, sometimes many of the gang members came over to Willibrord to harass us. If it hadn't been for Mr. Weston marching outside our school each day to protect us, the gang members probably would've robbed us blind.

"No," I told Mu'dear, hanging my head. "I don't wanna go to Carver."

Fortunately for me, I grew to enjoy the job. It gave me the opportunity to know many of the teachers on a more personal level. And sometimes, especially during the summer and winter breaks, Mr. Weston granted me free use of the gym to play basketball.

Mr. Christianson was a kind man, and he patiently taught me the skills of his trade. After getting over the initial shame, it felt good to work hard and to receive my education without resorting to charity.

Our eviction didn't prevent us from attending church. Every Sunday, we journeyed to Omega Missionary Baptist Church. It required several bus rides and a ride on the El—Chicago's train system. It took almost two hours to get there, and I'd usually fall asleep before we arrived.

Following church the first Sunday after our eviction, I watched out the window as we passed through some nice city neighborhoods. Families hung out on their porches and kids played in the yards. *Why can't we live like that again?*

Before returning to Granny's, we headed over to our old neighborhood to see the Faulkners; they were keeping our mail for us. When we departed the bus at South Bishop, I saw my home. It was boarded up; large sheets of plywood covered the windows. Seeing the windows made my stomach churn. We approached the house. *I hope no one sees us.* The padlock still secured the door, and the orange sticker still screamed, "No Trespassing."

People in the community worked hard to maintain their homes and yards. But our house looked like the city had condemned it. The Browns had brought down the value of the neighborhood.

Several months later, Mrs. Faulkner told Mu'dear that someone had purchased our place. The new owners even built a garage on the side yard. I couldn't imagine anyone living in our home—the home Dad built just for us.

That night as I lay on Granny's floor, I recalled the day we moved to South Bishop—I replayed how I'd admired the new furniture and how I'd raced upstairs to see my new room and bunk bed. *How dare other people move into our home. They're nothing more than thieves.*

But a few days later, I came home from school to find Mu'dear sitting at Granny's kitchen table and smiling. "I found us a new home!" She had accumulated enough money—with the help of living at Granny's for no rent and through my job at Willibrord—to place a security deposit and first month's rent on a house. "And," Mu'dear said, "it's bigger than our old home."

"No way!" I couldn't believe it. It was the best news I'd received in a very long time.

But then I learned Johnny wouldn't be living with us, and that tempered my joy.

chapter ten

THE LIFE OF A NOMAD

"For a just man falleth seven times, and then will rise again. — Proverbs 24:16

John was on a mission; he wanted to finish school, go to college, and then come back and save the family. He didn't think Mu'dear could provide the stability he needed to accomplish his goals. Granny was stable. She worked hard. She didn't earn a lot of money, but she held herself to a tight budget. Plus, Granny and John still enjoyed that special bond they'd created during John's first few years.

So Johnny stayed behind at Granny's, and we moved to a house near the intersection of 103rd and Wentworth. I missed my brother, but I was more focused on getting comfortable in our new home and making new friends. Fortunately, John and I made time to visit each other every day at school.

The house on Wentworth was indeed bigger than our home on Bishop. It was closer to Willibrord, and there was a good elementary school in the area for the girls. Mu'dear signed a lease contract with an option to buy, and she intended to buy it within a year or two. The owner also wanted it sold.

Purchasing another place sounded impossible given our circumstances. But Mu'dear said, "God will show us the way." She'd told the truth on the application. Our landlord knew about our finances. *Maybe God will make it work.*

When we moved in, Mu'dear hung a picture by the front door. It contained a photograph of a beach and the words to the famous poem by Mary Stevenson, *Footprints in the Sand*. The poem talked about God literally carrying us during the most difficult times in our lives. That's the way Mu'dear felt about our eviction. God had carried us through leaving our home and moving to Granny's, and now he'd set us down safely in our new home. I liked the area. Both Gwen and I had good friends in the neighborhood. I envisioned living there until I moved away for college.

A benefit of John staying at Granny's was that Gwen and I got to develop our relationship further. We talked until late in the evening—sharing our dreams with each other. And we talked about the nice things we'd buy Mu'dear when we made our fortunes. We'd buy her a big house with no mortgage, a new car, and we'd send her on trips to exotic locations.

Even though I questioned Mu'dear's sanity at times, I knew she was dedicated to serving us. Her friends, like Claudette, Linda, and Tyrone, came down hard on her, though. "You're just being lazy," one of them would say. "You need to get a job," said another.

"I am doing my job," Mu'dear told her friends. "God put me on this earth to be a mother. When I meet my maker, I want him to say that I served his children well."

Increasingly, Mu'dear's service extended to many

other people besides just her family and lifelong friends. Now, people she met in the neighborhood, or through other daily interactions, stopped by to unburden their hearts. They would call ahead or come by unannounced. Either way, Mu'dear made time to listen. She never judged. When they finished speaking, she inspired them to change their circumstances. "You don't have to accept the hand you've been dealt. Have a vision for something better. You can't be what you can't see."

All sorts of people sought my mother's listening ear: a man suffering from obesity, a woman enduring spousal abuse, a man hiding the fact he was gay, a woman ailing with cancer. As I often did, I sat nearby and eavesdropped on their conversations. *Where's she getting this wisdom? She's only twenty-nine.*

I worried that those troubled people might cause Mu'dear problems—that they might be a bad influence. Inspirational people attracted me, but people needing inspiration attracted Mu'dear. To be honest, sometimes I thought the whole thing was bizarre.

One day I asked her, "Why do all these people have to talk with *you*? I'm not sure it's good for you to hang around them."

"You can't judge people. You have to meet them where they are." She smiled. "Listen, Kenny. I've made plenty of mistakes, and you will, too. It's not our place to condemn others."

In a way, her listening ears and wise words were her currency. One man who Mu'dear helped was a cab driver. He wasn't very clean, and his cab number was 34, so we kids called him Dirty Four. Dirty Four was an older man with jet-black skin, and he'd come by our house and talk to Mu'dear for hours. In exchange, Dirty Four often provided us with free transportation.

Other people she helped loaned us money. And sometimes they would borrow it. Each month after we picked up our welfare check, Mu'dear gave ten percent to Omega Church, and then $10 to this person in need or $25 to that person. By the third week of the month, we'd run out of money, and other people would give Mu'dear $10 or $25.

"How can you let people take food out of our mouths?" I asked her.

Other family members wondered the same thing. "How can you not work, and then give your welfare money away?" they'd ask. "That's crazy."

"I can't beat God giving," she said, meaning she could never outgive God.

Mu'dear was like the woman in the Bible who gave her last two coins to the synagogue's treasury. Mu'dear didn't worry about running out; she trusted God to provide for our needs. And usually the money she gave away came back to her. Just not always by the same people.

But the money Mu'dear received still didn't cover our housing expenses. Once again, she fell behind in our house payments. Our landlord, realizing we couldn't realistically afford to buy our home, decided we needed to leave. He cancelled our contract.

Mu'dear knew she had no choice, and she found us another home. On a bright summer Saturday, one year after moving in, we cleared out the house and loaded up the rental truck. At least this time, we could take the belongings we had accumulated. One of the last things we removed was the *Footprints in the Sand* picture. *If God's still hanging around, it's time for him to carry us again.*

Our next house was a rental house near the intersection of 127th and Ashland. It was a brick, four-bedroom home—and bigger than the one before. It reminded me a lot of our neighborhood on South Bishop: wide streets, manicured lawns, and nearby parks. In fact, it was near Calumet Park, where the white boys chased me during my first year of elementary school. Geographically, we'd come almost full circle.

Mu'dear demonstrated her enduring faith by hanging the *Footprints* picture back up by the front door. But I questioned whether we'd ever break out of the cycle we were in. Once again, a landlord had accepted Mu'dear's application, but I knew nothing had changed in terms of our income. Mu'dear could've found a small apartment, but she insisted living in a full-size house. She wanted us to experience a normal home—not a tiny apartment, or worse, the projects.

But a few months later, the cycle started all over again. We got behind on payments. The electric and gas companies shut off our utilities. Then we received the eviction notice. After a couple of rounds through the court system, the sheriff's department once again threw us out. It was just a few weeks before Christmas break of my junior year.

All of our spirits, including Mu'dear's, took a beating. We were too embarrassed to even salvage our belongings, so we left them behind. We grabbed a few bags of clothing and boarded the bus.

I was too worn out to cry, but Mu'dear sobbed. "There are no accidents," she said, encouraging herself. "God doesn't make messes. He doesn't make messes."

She's in denial. I knew what others thought about her—she was either lazy or crazy. *Maybe they're right. We're like Israelites wandering around the wilderness. We're nomads.*

Mu'dear focused on reaching the Promised Land, but I grew exhausted from constantly moving my tent.

Granny's oldest child, Sonny, was a man with an entrepreneurial spirit. In the early 70s, he helped manage the singing group, The Dells, who were popular at the time. Later, he opened a clothing store called *La Roc's Boutique*. When record stores grew in popularity, he closed his clothing store and opened a record shop.

Sonny didn't have much education, especially in business management. He didn't keep any accounting records and walked around with wads of money in his pocket. The record store didn't survive, so he started another clothing shop, this one simply called *Sonny's*. He carried tailored women's clothing and shoes. He lived in a small area in the back, which he'd set up as a bedroom.

Although he didn't have much business sense, he possessed a strong desire to try new things. When the storefront next door became vacant, he leased it and put a doorway between the two shops. In the new space he opened an ice cream store. Unfortunately for him, that business didn't last, either. But the space offered an opportunity for shelter for us.

"Why don't you come over here," Uncle Sonny told Mu'dear when we were forced to leave 127th and Ashland. "You can stay in the back of the empty place. It's nothing fancy, but at least you'll have heat."

A few days before Christmas 1982, we moved into the back area of Uncle Sonny's defunct ice cream shop. The room was small, but it had carpeting, a refrigerator, and a hot plate for cooking soups.

For the next few days, we mostly talked. "How are you feeling?" Mu'dear asked often. Or, "What are you thinking about?"

I never hesitated to answer. "I'm wondering what God has against us. I keep passing those beautiful homes on the way home from church, and I don't understand why we have to keep moving."

"I don't know why, either. I don't know what God's plan is for us."

"It's not fair. What's the difference between us and other people? Maybe we're supposed to live like this."

"No! We can't become comfortable with this situation."

On Christmas Eve, Sonny walked up the street to Walgreen's Drug Store to buy a Christmas tree. He returned with a small fake tree—and a man.

"This is Thomas," Sonny said. "I met him at the Walgreen's and invited him for dinner."

Thomas looked like a homeless man. He'd been hitchhiking through the area and had nowhere to stay. When Sonny had arrived at the drug store, some other men were harassing Thomas. Sonny intervened and invited him back to the store. Like Mu'dear and Brother, Sonny was generous almost to a fault.

Chuckling, I said to Gwen, "Uncle Sonny's as crazy as Mu'dear." I was only half joking.

That night we sat on the carpet in the back and stayed up late, eating, talking, and laughing—a hobo, a homeless family, and a store owner with little business sense but an enormous heart. Sonny's girlfriend Miss Pearl also joined us.

A few weeks later, the landlord repossessed the ice

cream store. He boarded up the doorway between the two shops and padlocked the front door.

  We were on the move once again.

chapter eleven

ENDING UP
ON 79TH STREET

"Experience is not what happens to you, it is what you
do with what happens to you." — Aldous Huxley

We left Uncle Sonny's store and, carrying our bags of clothing, we walked three blocks to the apartment of Sonny's girlfriend—Miss Pearl. Clutching our coat collars against our necks to keep warm, we trudged past the liquor stores, pawnshops, and check cashing centers that populated 79th Street; the same street that Dad warned us about when he disapproved of our actions.

"Don't be a lumpkin," he said. "Do you want to end up on 79th Street someday?"

Now, that's exactly where we'd ended up.

We approached Ashland Avenue, and Miss Pearl met us and led us up to her apartment. A metal green security gate covered her front door. She jingled her keys, looking for the right set. First she unlocked a big silver padlock on the gate, then she unbolted the gate itself, and after sliding it open, she unlocked the door.

Her place was a small, one-bedroom apartment. She'd filled it with antiques—old tables and Victorian-looking chairs—and had covered the sofa in plastic. Dainty porcelain figurines sat on the end tables.

Miss Pearl pointed to a corner where we could place our belongings. She turned and smiled wearily. Two of her front teeth were capped in gold. She spoke in a genteel southern accent. "It isn't much. But please make yourselves at home."

Miss Pearl stood ramrod straight and folded her hands in front of her. Her fingernails were nicely polished. She was proper and polite.

I glanced away from her and through the bars of her living room window. *It's not fair that we have to move around like this. But this isn't fair to Miss Pearl, either. We're intruders.* I knew she didn't really want us there. She'd fallen in love with my uncle, but I'm sure she never expected us as part of the deal. Her apartment was no place for four children.

The next day, Gwen and I left the apartment at six in the morning to catch the CTA bus to school. A streetlamp hung over the bus stop, providing a dim yellow light against the darkness. It would take three buses and an El train to get to Willibrord. Gwen and I huddled close together and scanned the area for anyone strange coming near. Only a few hours earlier, the gangs and drug dealers had probably claimed the corner where we stood. My heart beat faster as I spotted a man in a heavy black coat walking toward us. As he approached, I could tell he was an older man. He stopped at the dry cleaner's behind us, opened the large gate that protected the entrance to the store, and went inside. A few moments later, he stepped back outside with a broom and swept up the collection of broken bottles that littered the sidewalk in front of his door.

Seventy-ninth Street was a main artery for the bus system, and we watched several buses go by before ours finally arrived. Gwen and I jumped on and took our seats among the bleary-eyed adults heading to work. I sighed in relief.

By the time we made it home from school, it was dark again. Uncle Sonny was visiting at Miss Pearl's, and he stayed and joined us for dinner. Uncle Sonny was often over, not only to visit with his girlfriend, but also to check on us and make sure we had everything we needed.

"I'm sorry the store didn't work out," he told me.

One Saturday, Sonny came over and brought along his dog Jake. He was a mid-size, brown dog with pointy ears. "Take him for a walk, will ya?" Sonny asked me.

I agreed, and Jake and I headed out the door.

Jake walked ahead, tugging on the leash. We passed the liquor store and the storefront church. The street was filled with buses, cars, and the sound of honking horns, so we turned on Ashland to get away from the noise. A block away, we found an empty lot, and I led Jake to it.

Suddenly, I spotted two guys strutting straight toward me. They looked to be around eighteen years old. One guy's hands were balled up in fists; the other stuck out his lower jaw.

Uh oh. I considered running.

"Hey, you!" one guy shouted.

I turned away, hoping they would leave, or I'd spot someone else they were talking to. No one else was around.

I tugged on Jake's leash. "Come on, Jake. Let's get outta here." But he was doing his business and wouldn't budge.

I can't leave him behind. Uncle Sonny'd kill me!

I could hear the men's footsteps getting closer.

"Move, Jake!" I tried dragging him.

"Hey! Don't go nowhere!" The two men ran up to me and surrounded me. One of the guys pushed me in the shoulder blades.

I spun around and saw a tall man with a wide nose.

"That's my dog," he said.

"No, it's not." My voice trembled. "It's my uncle's dog."

"Give it to me. It's mine."

"No. It's my—"

The guy punched me in the stomach. I collapsed to my knees in the dirt and gasped for air. I felt the leash ripped from my hand, but I couldn't do anything. I fell face first on the ground and tried not to vomit.

Oh, no. I lost Uncle Sonny's dog.

Breathing rapidly, I glanced behind me to see the two men dragging Jake away. *Uncle Sonny's gonna kill me.*

After a minute or so, I pushed myself up and walked back to Miss Pearl's. Halfway there, I caught my breath enough to run.

"Uncle Sonny! Uncle Sonny!" I burst through the front door, still holding my stomach.

Sonny jumped up from the plastic-covered sofa. "What's wrong?"

"They took the dog, Sonny. They took the dog." I said.

"What? Slow down. What are you talking about?"

"Two guys. Took Jake."

His eyes narrowed in a fierce glare. "Where? Where he at?"

I led him back to the vacant lot. From there, I spotted the two men standing on the porch of a nearby house. "That's them," I said pointing in their direction.

Sonny stormed off toward the men, and I followed. I didn't see Jake. We stopped at the porch steps, and Sonny asked me, "Which one is it? Which one stole my dog?"

I pointed at the tall man with the wide nose. "Him."

Sonny bounded up the stairs and grabbed the man by the collar. He slapped the man across the face several times. "Where's my dog? What's wrong with you?" The guy tried to break away, but Sonny wouldn't let go. Sonny shoved him against the house. "Where he at?"

"Around back," the man mumbled.

"Don't ever touch my property again! You don't touch my dog. And you don't touch my nephew. Got it?"

Sonny stormed inside the house, found the guy's mother in the kitchen, and told her what had happened. She screamed at her son.

In the backyard, we found about ten dogs. "They're probably all stolen," Sonny said. He grabbed Jake, and we walked home.

Sonny was a tough guy. You had to be if you lived on 79th Street. Despite our situation, I liked hanging around Sonny. By now, Dad had moved to New York, so Sonny filled a void and taught me a lot about being a man.

I still got to see Dad, though. When he could scrape together enough money, he'd send me an airline ticket, and I'd visit him for a long weekend or a week. The first time I flew on a plane, I sat nervously in the front row, fingering the wings pin the stewardess had given me. As the plane took off, I looked out the window and watched the city of Chicago disappear. Before we rose above the clouds, I studied the farmland and the seemingly endless stretches of trees and grass.

It wasn't long before I settled back in my seat. *I like this.*

Mu'dear often said I could only be as far as I could see. Up in the plane, I could see real far. *This is the way I want to live. I want to be somebody when I get older.*

Once in New York, Dad showed me all the sights, like the Empire State Building, the Statue of Liberty, and Madison Square Garden. We jogged in Central Park, and he took me to eat at his favorite Ethiopian restaurant. Later when he moved to Washington, D.C., and then California, I visited those places, too. In D.C., I toured the Capitol and other historic buildings, and in California, Dad took me to watch the Rose Bowl Parade.

Dad was as intense as he'd always been. He encouraged me to read and improve myself. "Knowledge is the mark of a real man."

His leaving still angered me. "How can you stand living so far away from your family?" I asked once.

"It's not easy. But I'm doing what I'm supposed to be doing. I'm living in my purpose."

I can't say that answer helped much, but I still knew he loved me. He called often and stayed connected with my life. It didn't hurt, either, that every time I visited Dad, he exposed me to new and wonderful experiences.

In addition to Dad and Sonny, however, there were other people who helped me grow into manhood. Three people, in particular, come to mind.

During the summer after my junior year, I found a job through CEDA—the City Educational Development Authority in Chicago. The city government had established and funded the program to provide low-income youth with summer jobs. They hired college and high school-age kids to clean parks, do landscaping work, or work in summer camps. During the summer of 1983, I was lucky enough to work a job at St. Thaddeus Elementary School, which hosted a camp for elementary school kids.

At the camp, I met two men—Richard Gardner and Shawn Moore. Both of them attended college and came from inner-city backgrounds similar to mine. Right away, I recognized something special in them. They both carried themselves confidently, and I just knew they were headed toward a bright future. Sometimes, they wore black t-shirts with gold, Greek lettering on them. I didn't understand what the letters represented, but I figured it had something to do with their college activities.

Richard worked as a camp counselor, and Shawn was an assistant like me. Whenever Richard spoke to the kids, I sat and listened—mesmerized by his words of inspiration. "You can be whatever you want to be," he told them. Many of the children had witnessed terrible things in their young lives, but Richard encouraged them to let nothing stop them from learning and succeeding.

"You're an ambassador of hope," I told Richard.

Until that time, I hadn't thought much about college—except that I knew Mu'dear would kill me if I didn't go. But those two guys made me think about it more. *I want to go to college and be like them.* Little did I know that they'd play important roles in my life during future years.

Some of the faculty at Willibrord also helped me grow into manhood. Of course, our principal Mr. Weston set a great example, as did other teachers. But the teacher who probably helped me most was also the most unlikely. That teacher was a short little nun we called Twitch.

Sister Teresa was an older Caucasian lady who taught English. She was around five feet tall and walked with a limp—she sort of twitched when she walked down the hall, which is how she got her nickname. The first day of class, she made us act out a scene from *Romeo and Juliet.* "Ken Brown. You'll play the role of Escalus. Go up front."

I didn't feel good that day—I was probably tired from sleeping on Miss Pearl's floor. "Do I have to?" Sister Teresa immediately twitched herself over to me; her black polished shoes clicking on the wood floor.

"Don't be a sissy," she said, grabbing my earlobe. She pulled me to the front of the room. "Be a man, Mr. Brown."

I began reading Escalus's part.

"No, no, no," she said. "Show emotion. Get inside the character. Remember this Mr. Brown, in this classroom our motto is: 'Excellence or nothing at all.'"

I didn't care much for Sister Twitch that first day. But I grew to love her. And I grew to love literature because of her. Dad had insisted that we read Plato, Dickens, and Shakespeare, and I'd done it grudgingly. But Twitch motivated me to understand those works and be moved by them. We acted out most of the stories we read. She made it fun, while insisting we put everything into our efforts. She stuck to her creed of excellence.

Toward the end of the year, she made us memorize a poem. The poem was titled, *If,* and was written by Rudyard Kipling. "Don't ever forget this poem," she said.

One day, I stood in the front of the class and recited it:

"If you can keep your head when all about you
Are losing theirs and blaming it on you;
If you can trust yourself when all men doubt you,
But make allowance for their doubting too;
If you can wait and not be tired by waiting,
Or, being lied about, don't deal in lies,
Or, being hated, don't give way to hating,
And yet don't look too good, nor talk too wise;

If you can dream—and not make dreams your master;
If you can think—and not make thoughts your aim;
If you can meet with Triumph and Disaster
And treat those two impostors just the same;
If you can bear to hear the truth you've spoken
Twisted by knaves to make a trap for fools,
Or watch the things you gave your life to broken,
And stoop and build 'em up with worn-out tools;

If you can make one heap of all your winnings
And risk it on one turn of pitch-and-toss,
And lose, and start again at your beginnings
And never breathe a word about your loss;
If you can force your heart and nerve and sinew
To serve your turn long after they are gone,
And so hold on when there is nothing in you
Except the Will which says to them: "Hold on;"

If you can talk with crowds and keep your virtue,
Or walk with kings—nor lose the common touch;
If neither foes nor loving friends can hurt you;
If all men count with you, but none too much;
If you can fill the unforgiving minute
With sixty seconds' worth of distance run—
Yours is the Earth and everything that's in it,
And—which is more—you'll be a Man, my son!"

Kipling's words grabbed me like none I'd ever read before:

"If you can keep your head when all about you are losing theirs," "If you can trust yourself when all men doubt you," "If you can meet with Triumph or Disaster and meet those two imposters just the same...."

They made me think of how Mu'dear had kept her head through all our trials.

And how Dad had trusted himself to grow and learn.

And about the disasters my family had faced and survived, still clinging to a brighter future.

The poem gave me a guide to manhood—and the confidence to know my childhood trials would serve me well in the future.

chapter twelve

PEEKING OVER
THE FENCE

"There is nothing like a dream to create the future."
— Victor Hugo

Mu'dear got wise and found us a smaller place to live—an apartment at 71ˢᵗ and Crandon Streets. It was a two-bedroom place on the eighth floor—much tighter quarters than we were use to, but it was near the lakefront and had a nice view of the water. To make ends meet, Mu'dear made and sold baskets and cooked dinners for other people. We still scraped by on thin bologna sandwiches and government cheese, but we were able to stay in the apartment for my entire senior year.

The building had a doorman, and it reminded me of the hotel Dad use to work in. On television, I loved the show *Hotel*, which took place in an ornate hotel in San Francisco. My favorite character was Peter McDermott, the sophisticated general manager of the hotel. Many people in my family had worked in the hospitality industry, and more and more, I saw myself working in the same area someday. Even if they didn't work in hospitality, people in my family—Mu'dear, Dad, my uncles—committed themselves to serving others. *I want do the same thing.*

My best friend Mark was in my homeroom class, and he talked often about the colleges he was considering. Southern Illinois University, in particular, interested him.

"Have you started looking yet?" Mark asked.

He always had a concern for other people; he had a gentle, fun-loving spirit. Everybody loved him. In fact, at the end of the year, our class voted him the Best Male Personality.

The girl we voted Best Personality was Deidre Coats, who was also in my homeroom class. Mark sat beside me, and Deidre behind me. Deidre had a plan for everything, and she often asked me what my plans for college were.

It's time to get serious about my future.

Willibrord Catholic High School was run under the auspices of the St. Norbertine order. One day, Brother Matthew, who was on staff at the school, gathered the seniors together in the cafeteria. "I'm working on a project with our brothers in Green Bay, Wisconsin. Our order sponsors a college there, the College of St. Frances. The school's trying to attract minority students and has invited any senior from this school to a weekend retreat in Green Bay. You'll stay with a family and tour the school. We'll cover all your expenses."

I was stoked. *A retreat! A chance to get away.* Like traveling to visit Dad, I jumped at the opportunity to get out of the inner city. I asked Mu'dear for permission to go on the trip, and because it was about college, she quickly agreed.

Brother Matthew drove ten of us on a van to Wisconsin.

We got stuck in Friday afternoon traffic, but slowly we made it out of the concrete jungle, and headed up I-94 through the suburbs, and then through the cornfields and cow pastures. I couldn't help but smile as we traveled through the countryside. But I kept silent—playing it cool and acting as if seeing another world was no big deal.

However, the guy next to me, Jeffrey, couldn't contain his joy. "Man, oh, man," he said, shaking his head. "Man, oh, man. I can't believe I'm doing this."

"You ever seen the country before?" I asked.

"Nope. I never even leave the projects except to go to school." A tear rolled down his cheek, and he ignored it.

Jeffrey and his mother lived in the Cabrini Green Housing Project. His shirt was frayed at the edges, and his jacket was thin and threadbare at the elbows. He was as poor as I was, but where I didn't advertise my situation, Jeffrey did. He often talked about how little money he had—but in an innocent, matter-of-fact way. Jeffrey possessed such a childlike spirit, that our classmates loved him.

I observed him and experienced the excitement of the trip through him. He was tall, around six-foot-two, and wore large plastic glasses over his wide nose. More tears ran down along the rim of his glasses and his cheeks. "Man, oh, man," he kept repeating.

Around ten o'clock, we arrived in the town of Green Bay. Nobody was out. No cars lined the streets. No people walked the sidewalks. Chicago bustled with activity on a Friday night, but Green Bay seemed like a ghost town.

The lack of traffic and noise unsettled me. I took a deep breath. *Maybe this was a mistake.*

We pulled up to the school and got off the van. Nobody was there to greet us. Before we'd left, Brother

Matthew warned us that few minorities lived in the area. "You might get a few stares."

Maybe they decided they didn't want us after all.

The sidewalk was clean—not a scrap of paper or broken bottle in sight. Jeffrey looked around with his mouth hanging open. After ten minutes, a column of headlights approached from up the street. First a Corvette arrived, and then a Jeep Cherokee, a BMW, and a Cadillac. They pulled up behind the bus. All the drivers were young—and white.

"These are your hosts," Brother Matthew announced.

A young man introduced himself to me. "Hi, my name's David. It's great to meet you." We shook hands.

"There are no ground rules for the weekend," Brother Matthew said. "You'll stay with your host the whole time. The only requirement is that you take a tour of the college. Spend some time walking in the shoes of a college student."

David led me to his Corvette, and we got in. I glanced back at Jeffrey. He got into a BMW as he shook his head in amazement.

David drove me to his home, and we talked the whole way there. I learned that his father owned two Chevrolet dealerships in the area. David made several turns through a rustic subdivision with multi-acre lots, and then he veered off the road and down a long drive. The car vibrated as we rolled over the brick pavers of the circular driveway.

David lived in a huge ranch house surrounded by large shrubs and flowers. Ceiling-high windows ran across the front, giving a view all the way to the back of the house. We got out of the Corvette, and David opened the wooden double doors to his home.

We stepped in and his mother rushed up to greet me. "Well, hello, Kenneth. How are you doing?" She led me into the family room. "It's so wonderful to have you here." She talked to me for half an hour, like she had known me for years. David's father and brother also came and introduced themselves. The house smelled like oak, and a fire burned behind glass doors in the fireplace.

David took me down to the basement where his bedroom was located. His room was probably larger than my apartment. He had a huge stereo system, a big screen television, and a waterbed.

"You can sleep in my bed tonight," he said.

"Nah. Thanks, though." I didn't want to sleep in the waterbed. I couldn't swim, and I'd heard an old wives' tale that if the mattress burst, you could drown.

"I insist. You sleep in it."

I finally gave in, but I didn't sleep too well that night. However, I did enjoy feeling the warmth of the mattress, as well as the warmth of David's home and family. *This is the way I want to live.*

In the morning, I woke to the smell of fresh-baked bread. David and I went upstairs, and I saw the long kitchen table covered in dishes of scrambled eggs, fried potatoes, bacon, and muffins. The five of us ate breakfast and talked and laughed for over an hour.

Through the picture windows in the kitchen, I observed a glorious view of the lake. "Did you bring your swim trunks?" David asked.

"No. I don't swim."

"No matter. You can borrow mine."

After breakfast, David took me out to his boat, which was docked off the backyard. We pulled out into the lake and eventually met up with several other hosts and my classmates. Most of our hosts owned boats, and for three hours, they took several of my classmates water skiing. Neither Jeffrey nor I swam, so we hung out in the back of David's boat and talked.

"Man, this guy's got a maid," Jeffrey said about his host. "She cooked an incredible breakfast. They've got marble floors and cherry cabinets. His father's a brain surgeon." He started crying again. "I can't believe I'm getting to do this."

Later that afternoon, David took me on a tour of the college. I always imagined college as a stuffy place where people wore suits and shuffled through regimented lives. But at St. Frances, I saw students in t-shirts and jeans, or even pajamas, hanging out and talking, watching television, throwing Frisbees, and at times, studying. *This looks fun. I can really see myself in a place like this.*

At the end of the trip, I met with a representative from the school. He said that if they accepted me for admission, they'd offer me a full scholarship.

As Brother Matthew drove us home Sunday evening, I thought about my future. I'd spent a weekend seeing another world, and I liked what I saw. *I'd like to get away from Chicago for a while.* I'd always lived in somebody's shadow, whether it was Dad's, Mu'dear's, or John's. College would grant me some independence—a chance to chart my own path in life and see what I was made of.

Many people in the inner city, however, didn't support the idea of college. Dad warned me about people who had a ghetto mentality. "People think the ghetto is a place: the inner city, black folks, graffiti on the walls. But the ghetto is more of an attitude. It's hopelessness. And when people give up hope, they don't like to see other people succeed, because they know it reflects poorly on themselves. It's like crabs in a barrel."

"Crabs in a barrel?"

"Yeah. If you put two crabs in a barrel, inevitably one'll try to crawl out. Just as it sees the light of day, the other one will grab its claw and yank it back down. They'll both die because they work against each other."

When it came to college, a lot of people in the inner city projected a crab mentality. "Why do you want to waste your time on college?" a man who lived in our apartment building asked me. "I've known people who've gone to college, spent thousands of dollars, and come back home without a job. They end up stocking shelves at Blockbuster."

"Why do you wanna go away from Chicago?" a guy I played basketball with asked me. "You too good to stay in the city?"

I heard a lot of comments like those. But I remembered Dad's words. And I remembered all the things he exposed me to. And I remembered the houses Mu'dear moved us into and our visits to the Millionaire's Club. They helped me peek over the backyard fence. Now it was time to open the gate and live somewhere else.

But as I watched out the van window and saw us approaching Chicago, I knew I wouldn't go to St. Frances College. It was too different—too far away. As much as I desired to live somewhere new, I was also a person of associations. Family and friends meant a lot to me, and I needed to attend a school where I'd still feel connected.

Like Dad had talked about not having a ghetto mentality, Mu'dear talked about not having a welfare mentality. "Welfare is a bridge," she said. "It's not a way of life." Mu'dear viewed welfare as a resource for getting her family ahead, and she sought other resources as well. While I was trying to determine how to move ahead with college, she learned of a government counseling center that offered college advice to low-income students.

One day, I sat in the spartan office of one of the government counselors. I fidgeted; I was nervous and excited about going to school. I didn't speak as the counselor studied my transcripts.

He glanced at me and frowned. "Maybe you shouldn't attend college."

"What?" I shook my head quickly, trying to understand what he meant. He was supposed to help get me into college, not discourage me from even trying.

"Your grades aren't that good. You should probably focus on getting a trade."

It was true—I was basically a C student. But that wasn't going to stop me. "I'm going to college."

"You might not get in," he said.

You jerk. I clenched my jaw and resisted the temptation to storm out of his office. "Well, let's try."

The man grudgingly walked me through the process of applying for a Pell Grant and guaranteed loans. Then he listed some schools where the Pell Grant would cover most of the expenses. "There's Columbia, Chicago State, or the Illinois Institute of Technology." My brother John attended the Illinois Institute of Technology.

"Those are all city schools. Tell me about some schools outside Chicago."

"Okay, if you insist. The big three schools within a day's drive are Illinois State, Northern Illinois, and Southern Illinois." *Southern I. That's where Mark's looking.*

A month later, John drove Mark and me to SIU at

Carbondale for the weekend. John's ex-girlfriend Valerie attended SIU. She was real nice and led us on a tour of the campus. It was a large school, with around 25,000 students.

The sun reflected across a nearby lake, and a warm breeze blew over the campus. Groups of people played sports on fields of dark green grass. A group of black men played football, and guys from Spain played soccer. A collection of longhaired guys rode skateboards down the sidewalk.

We visited two tall dorm buildings, as well as the library, bookstore, and academic buildings. While walking around, I ran into Gretchen Hilliard, who was the sister of a friend of mine from elementary school.

I immediately felt comfortable at SIU. In fact, I felt like I'd been there before, even though I never had.

When we finished with the tour, I thanked Valerie for spending so much time with us. *I've found a home.* It was just far enough from Chicago, had a beautiful campus, and—through Valerie and Gretchen—I already had connections. And maybe Mark would go there, too.

When I returned to homeroom on Monday, I told Deidre that I was going to try for SIU.

"Hey," she said. "That's where I'm going!"

It was no accident that Deidre and I would attend the same college.

chapter thirteen

THE MIRACLE OF COLLEGE

"A small decision now can change all your tomorrows."
— Robert Schuller

I don't know how she did it, but Mu'dear scrounged up enough money to pay for my senior class trip to Orlando, Florida. I think Uncle Sonny had something to do with it. Mu'dear wouldn't tell me, though, and I was afraid I'd jinx things if I asked too much.

"You deserve this," Mu'dear said. "Go and have fun."

Mark and I, along with other friends, enjoyed an exciting time in Orlando—going to Disney World, Epcot Center, and other places. While there, a friend of mine, Ken Walker, tried to win over a girl by the name of Kimberly. Kimberly was a friend of Deidre's, and they hung out together on the trip.

"Why don't you and Deidre hang out with Kim and me?" Ken asked. "That way Kim can get to know me without too much pressure."

I agreed. I didn't have any romantic interest in Deidre, but I always enjoyed talking with her. During the trip, the four of us spent a lot of time together.

After we returned home, Ken and Kim dated, and the four of us took picnics at the lake. Deidre and I sat on the rocks and talk about the future—she wanted to be a teacher, and I wanted to run a restaurant. I even talked to her about the girls I hoped to date.

In the fall of 1983, I officially applied to Southern Illinois. But as I waited for a response, I dwelled on the comments of that government counselor. "Your grades aren't that good. You might not get in."

Despite his pessimism, I had to admit he had a point. So, before I ended up receiving a rejection letter, I called the school. "Look, I know my grades aren't what they should be. But you know what? I know I can excel if you give me a shot." I spent fifteen minutes telling the school's representative how I'd let nothing stand in my way of getting good grades. "Is there any way I can show you what I can do?"

"Oh yeah," he said, "We have a special admissions program we reserve for students who show promise. You have to earn at least a B average during your freshman year, and then we'll process you through general admissions."

"Can you sign me up?"

I must have impressed him with my commitment. "Absolutely," he said.

A month later, I received a notice of probationary acceptance to SIU. *Now it's on!*

As graduation approached, Deidre passed me notes in homeroom about her preparations for SIU: "I bought a television for my room yesterday." "I got a radio." "I bought some towels and a comforter."

"What's a comforter?" I hadn't bought anything. I didn't have the money, so I spent little time preparing for college. All I cared about was making a new start.

But it was fun to plan our future in college. By then, Mark had also committed to SIU, and I knew it would be a blessing to go to school with such good friends.

Mark and I decided to room together, and we made that request on our enrollment forms. I didn't have the money for the enrollment fee, however. The form stated that if the fee was not received by the deadline, then the school wouldn't provide housing.

"Just have faith and send in the form," Mu'dear said. "Everything'll work out."

I'm getting tired of this faith thing. The constant need to depend on faith, and not funds, wore me down. "Isn't there any way we can come up with the money?"

But I knew the answer. We were going through the same old struggle at home. Utilities were being cut off, and the landlord called often to demand back pay. *Maybe I shouldn't have gone to Florida.*

The deadline passed for the fee, and Mu'dear repeated her encouragement. "Just go to school and have faith."

In August of 1984, Mark's dad drove the two of us to SIU. I brought with me $25 and a white wicker chair. As we drove along Route 57, I watched the countryside pass by and thought about my plane trips and my road trip to Green Bay. But this trip was different. I closed my eyes, feeling the warm sunshine on my face. I didn't plan on going home to visit much. My old life had ended, and I was anxious to test myself and see what I was made of.

My housing situation, however, kept me from indulging in unrestrained excitement. I'd survived four years of upheaval, and now I craved a stable place to live. *I'm probably going to end up in communal housing with eight other people.*

We arrived on the SIU campus and parked outside of Allen Hall—Mark's dormitory building. He was in room 320. I left Mark and his dad and walked to the housing office.

I introduced myself to the woman at the front desk and waited nervously for her to tell me my situation. "Let's see, Mr. Brown," she said, looking up my records. "We have a room for you."

"What?" I couldn't believe it.

"Yes, you have financial aid coming, so we went ahead and assigned you one. It's in Allen Hall."

That's Mark's building!

She handed me a key. Attached to it was a strip of masking tape, and on the tape was written: "319." *I'm next door to Mark?*

I walked out of the housing office in a daze. I stopped and stared across campus to Allen Hall. Getting that room next to Mark triggered a realization. Tears welled up. *Mu'dear's faith is real.*

I glanced around at the campus and grasped that, under normal circumstances, I wasn't supposed to be there. I was a child of teenage, out-of-wedlock parents. I was a welfare recipient. An inner-city nomad.

But while facing a chorus of disapproval from family and friends, Mu'dear had persisted. *Mu'dear's faith got me to college. This is a miracle.*

I returned to Allen Hall and settled in my room. After Mark's dad drove away, Mark and I looked at each other and sighed.

"Whoooo," I said, letting out a long breath. I had my freedom. I had a room, with lights, heat, and a telephone.

It was mine for the next four years. I had a network of connections through Mark, Deidre, Valerie, and Gretchen. I had a chance to make my own way—to be the captain of my fate.

And I had faith. A faith—gifted by my mother—that promised a bright future.

"You can only be as far as you can see," Mu'dear had said. I scanned the campus—the lake and the fields of newly-arrived students—and gazed at the horizon. *I can see real far.*

My roommate came from the west side of Chicago. He was around six-foot-four and muscular—a football player. He wore the same green shorts almost every day and rarely showered. He didn't talk much, which was difficult for me, since talking was one of my favorite activities.

Fortunately for me, I lived next door to Mark. We kept our doors open most of the time, and spent most of our study time together. Mark's roommate was a guy who liked to wear the nicest clothes and party a lot. He and Mark connected about as poorly as my roommate and I, but for some reason, our two roommates hit it off great. A few months into the school year, they approached us about switching roommates. We quickly agreed.

Mark and I were roommates! Another miracle.

College life introduced me to people from all over the world. People from Asia and Europe attended SIU. And there were African-Americans from Chicago and Caucasians from smaller towns like Murphysboro and Peoria. Some of the white students had never eaten with a black person prior to our first meal in the dining hall.

At first, blacks and whites stayed in their own groups.

But then baseball brought us together. During the fall of '84, the Chicago Cubs competed in a heated race for the National League East Division Championship. The Cubs hadn't made it to the playoffs in almost forty years.

As we watched the games on the big screen in the student lounge, blacks and whites sat on opposite sides of the room. But as the baseball season reached its culmination, we got to know each other, and we started sitting together—African-Americans and Caucasians on the same sofas.

With one week to go in the season, the Cubs beat the Pirates 4-1 and clinched their first division championship since 1945. We celebrated as one group. We'd come together for a common goal. Afterward, we ran around campus cheering and rolling trees with toilet paper.

But other than watching baseball and a few other sports, I didn't watch much television. I studied hard. I needed to get through the year with at least a B average—if I didn't, the school would send me packing.

Mark, on the other hand, didn't spend much time studying; he was naturally smart. He followed a disciplined schedule and completed his work quickly each afternoon. He was a real math whiz and could grasp complex problems with, what seemed to me, little effort. We complemented each other well: he was a thinker; I was a doer.

Sometimes, I struggled with my work and doubted whether I could achieve the grades I needed. My family's situation at home also weighed on me; they'd been evicted once again and had moved into another apartment.

But Mark encouraged me. He saw something special in me. "Ken Brown, great things are going to happen to you. I see how hard you're working. You've got drive and determination." Mark was a Ken Brown fan. "You're going to go places," he said.

And of course, I was a Mark Burrell fan. I admired his intellect and his unconditional friendship. I depended on his support that first year.

After being best friends for five years, I thought Mark would always be there for me.

Mark and I maintained our friendship with Deidre. On weekend evenings, she often hung out in our room. The three of us popped popcorn, watched television, and talked. Other times, Mark and I hung around Deidre's room. Mark had attended elementary school with Deidre's roommate, Pam, so the four us made a comfortable group.

Mark usually went to bed before me, so if Deidre was over when he turned in, she and I moved to the lounge down the hall. She dated a man at SIU, and I still dated a lady back in Chicago, and we talked about our relationships—what was going right and wrong. Words flowed easily between us. We talked late into the evening, and inevitably, the conversation would lighten up and we'd get giddy with laughter.

Mark admired her as much as I did. "That, Dee," he said. "She's something special. Isn't she sweet?"

"Yeah. She's great," I said. "A true friend."

But one night as Deidre and I talked in the lounge, a new feeling came over me. She sat on the sofa and talked, and I stood across from her. I can be impulsive, and I suddenly felt an urge to kiss her. I hadn't planned anything in advance, but I felt such a strong connection with her, and I got caught up in the moment.

As she talked, I walked over to her, bent over, and kissed her. She kissed me back. *Wow.*

My skin tingled.

I kissed her again.

I can't believe this is happening.

It may sound corny, but after that, I knew Deidre and I were meant to be together. The next day, we ended our other relationships. I knew I didn't have a choice in the matter. I couldn't see myself with anyone else.

Ever.

chapter fourteen

A TIME FOR GROWTH AND REFLECTION

"Unless you try to do something beyond what
you have already mastered, you will never grow."
— Ronald Osborne

I finished my freshman year with a 3.15 Grade Point Average, and SIU accepted me into full admission. With some of the pressure off, I decided to investigate the Greek fraternities on campus. I thought a fraternity would help me chart a new course for my life. My brother John had considered joining a fraternity at IIT, but in the end, he opted not to.

This is an opportunity to do something different—something no one in my family has done.

During Rush week, I stopped by an exhibit for the Alpha Phi Alpha fraternity and approached a brother who was handing out information. *He looks familiar.* "Hi, I'm Ken Brown," I said as I tried to place him.

"Hey, Ken! I'm Shawn Moore. We worked together two years ago at the St. Thaddeus camp."

I couldn't believe it. Standing next to Shawn was Richard Gardner, the camp counselor I had so admired. They wore the same black shirts with Greek letters that I'd seen on them that summer.

Shawn and Richard explained to me that Alpha Phi Alpha was the oldest African-American Greek fraternity in the United States. It was started in 1906 at Cornell University and claimed many famous members, such as Thurgood Marshall, Martin Luther King Jr., and Andrew Young. The founding members established the fraternity on the principles of academic excellence, fellowship, good character, and the uplifting of humanity. The four principles hit home for me and reminded me of my parents' values.

Running into Shawn and Richard must be some sort of sign. I need to be a part of this.

Later that week, I interviewed with a committee from the fraternity. They accepted me as a pledge—along with thirteen other men. But that was only the beginning of the process. I had to pass an eight-week pledge program that tested my endurance and commitment to the group.

"It's very difficult," Richard said. "Most people don't make it."

Richard was right. It was one of the most challenging eight weeks of my life. I wasn't allowed to talk—in person or on the phone—except when it was necessary for my classes. I had to literally run everywhere that I went. I had to wear a white dress shirt, black tie, and black pants. Worst of all, I couldn't socialize, including spending time with Deidre.

Dee supported me completely. In fact, she wanted to join a sorority but waited until the next semester so she could support me during my pledge period. She left notes on my desk or messages through Mark: "Hang in there!" or "I love you!" Sometimes, late at night, I'd sneak off and met her at the lake. We wouldn't talk, but hugged and kissed, and

I soaked up her love and support.

Being such an avid talker, it pained me to remain silent for so long. Many nights, I lay in bed and considered quitting. I felt dead by being silent. I missed Deidre. I missed talking to my family. But my experiences with evictions and poverty gave me fuel to persevere. I've been through worse. At least I know when this struggle will end.

I drew on my growing faith. I didn't know how to pray with eloquence, but I talked with God—just like I talked with Mu'dear.

"Don't worry." I felt him saying. "I carried you through the tough times of your childhood. I'll carry you now. You'll make it."

As the weeks wore on, I was surprised to occasionally enjoy the solitude. It slowed me down. I'd moved away from the drama of my life in Chicago, but I worked so hard my first year of college, I didn't take time to reflect on my past. Now, I took walks in a nearby woods and thought and prayed. The Holy Spirit had always flowed through me, I believed, but I'd been too busy to notice. I learned to slow down and connect with the presence of God.

A fraternity brother served as a pastor at Mt. Zion Baptist Church, and I started attending services at his church. As a child attending Omega Church, I asked God why I couldn't live in a nice home like other people. Now, I understood. He was teaching me to trust in him and to be strong through the tough times.

When the eight-week pledge period ended, only four of the original fourteen students remained. I was one of them.

As I walked into the ballroom for my initiation into Alpha Phi Alpha, I stopped short and stared at one of the people seated in the room. It was John!

My brother had hopped an Amtrak train to Carbondale to see my initiation. When I was younger, I stood in John's shadow. For him to surprise me by attending my initiation meant the world to me. I was now my own man.

"I'm very proud of you," he said with a smile and a hint of a tear.

Joining Alpha Phi Alpha proved to be one of the best things I could've done. The older brothers, like Shawn and Richard, mentored me and taught me skills I'd need in the working world. Richard was in a pre-med program and excelled in academics. To make sure we stayed committed to our education, he demanded to see our grades after each reporting period.

One time, I brought him a report card with a C in a math class. "Math is vital," he said. "Don't be afraid of it. If you need help, we'll get you a tutor. I expect this to be higher next semester."

He also taught us good study habits. He always seemed to study and had bloodshot eyes from his many late nights. He strove for excellence, and I learned a lot about excellence by observing him.

My fraternity brothers also prepared me for a world where racial prejudice still existed. "To make it in this world, you'll need the highest levels of personal integrity and quality."

To encourage us, they made us memorize several poems. I had no problem memorizing one of them—the poem, If. Once again, Rudyard Kipling's ode to manhood played a key role in my life. We recited it often during meetings. Kipling's message of perseverance, strength, vision, and humility centered me on the qualities required for success.

I only went back to Chicago a few times during my years at SIU, but I talked to Mu'dear often on the phone. As my sisters each moved on to college, Mu'dear's life stabilized. With all of us gone, the pressure lifted, and she held down a job. She found work as a domestic home care provider— someone who provides non-medical assistance to the sick or elderly. Two of her main responsibilities were to cook for her care receivers and to sit and talk with them—needless to say, she met the qualifications. Her job paid for her one-bedroom apartment, and after my last sister, Loretta, moved out, Mu'dear never faced eviction again.

When she wasn't serving the people she worked for, she continued to serve the people that came into her life every day. Her zeal to talk about God and help others grew so strong, that many people worried about her sanity.

One day I received a phone call from John. "I'm afraid Mu'dear's lost her mind. All she talks about is God. And now she's giving away most of her things."

"What do you mean giving away her things?"

"Her clothes. Her money. Even some of her furniture. If she thinks people are in trouble, she just gives it to them— no questions asked."

Somehow I wasn't surprised.

"Kenny, we might lose her. Something's seriously wrong with her. Some family members think we need to commit her, so she can get some help."

"Commit her? What're you talking about? People always thought she was crazy, but look at us. Look how we turned out."

"This is different. She's not acting like a rational person. I'm the oldest, and I think we need to commit her."

That weekend, I took the bus to Chicago. Mu'dear looked happy and vibrant, and she hugged me when I walked in her door.

"Do you know what people are saying about you?" I asked. "They say you're crazy, and they're talking about committing you to a hospital."

Mu'dear shook her head sadly. "Yes, I know."

"I believe in this faith thing, because I've walked with you. I've felt God carry us. But other people aren't feeling it. They don't think you're acting right in the head."

"Kenny, you understand. Don't you?"

"That's why I'm here, because I understand. But can't you tone it down a bit? Can't you show a little less zeal? Can't you keep some of your money and things? You were poor for so long. There's nothing wrong with holding on to some of the extra now that you have it."

Mu'dear wiped away tears. "No, Son. I can't be responsible for the beliefs of others. I know what I read in the Word, and I know what I feel in my heart. I have to be obedient."

Mu'dear stood her ground. She would not change. "The Word says that others will call you a fool for following him. So let them call me a fool."

After that conversation, I prayed often for God to protect her. *Please, Lord, guard her mind and help others to understand her.*

To this day, Mu'dear continues to serve others and live in obedience to God's guidance. While some people continued to question her wisdom, the thought of committing her never came up again.

Mu'dear's faith and servanthood set an example for me to follow. Since I liked people so much, I sometimes befriended fellow classmates who were struggling through difficult times. I didn't bring up my past unsolicited—I didn't want to become a poster child for welfare and food stamps—but if someone was hurting, I'd volunteer everything that I went through.

One guy who lived in my dorm often shared his problems. His name was Peter, and he suffered from low self-confidence. He wore Jeri curls, but he hadn't maintained them; his curls had flattened and his hair had turned from black to sandy red. He wore large glasses and acne dotted his face.

Peter complained about his family and financial situation. "We were always the poorest people in the neighborhood. Nobody ever helped us get ahead." His mother now called him every other day to unload bad news from home. "Mama just told me that my brother's been arrested again. You don't stand a chance in this world if you're black and poor."

"But, Pete," I said. "That's not true. You're here. Not back at home. The past is in the past."

"I can't let go of it. It's always on my mind. I feel like a failure."

"Listen, when you change your thoughts, you change your world. Don't let your family's situation suck you back down. You've got a bright future ahead of you. Stay positive."

He smiled. "I guess you're right."

But the next day, he wallowed in self-destructive thoughts again. He couldn't believe anything would ever change in his life. Eventually, Peter dropped out of school and went back home; he couldn't break away from his past. We came from similar backgrounds, but our attitudes separated us. An optimistic attitude, I learned, played a key role in keeping one on the right path.

Another person I talked to was a young woman I met through Mark. Her name was Judy, and she was a friend of Mark's girlfriend, Nanette. As a child, Judy witnessed her father stab and kill her mother. After that, the government sent her and her sisters to various foster homes. Judy, being the oldest, took over the mothering role.

Even though I'd never witnessed such violence, because of my background of instability, we related to each other. I listened to her, let her cry, and occasionally tried to convey some of the lessons my parents had imparted to me. "Trouble doesn't last forever. You're here now. You need a plan for the future." Unlike Peter, Judy earned her degree.

My best friend in the fraternity, Stephan Franklin, and I also came from similar backgrounds. He grew up in the inner city of Chicago and attended a Catholic school. We shared a lot about our childhoods and dreams for the future.

"One thing about you," Stephan once told me, "You're a great friend because you're transparent. You don't hide anything. And you help a lot of people that way."

His comments humbled me. I began to understand why the Bible says that everything works for good for those people who love God and follow his will. *I can use my past experiences as a source of strength—for myself and others.*

Unfortunately, my words weren't enough to help my buddy Mark. His girlfriend Nanette owned a moped, and occasionally she let Mark borrow it. One day, Mark returned from riding the bike and had blood dripping down his knee—he'd been in a minor accident. Over the next few days, his knee didn't heal, so his mother persuaded him to come home and visit their family doctor. While there, the doctor ran some blood tests on Mark and discovered that Mark's kidneys only functioned at half their capacity.

Mark called me a few days later. "It looks like I'm not coming back right away. I have to go on dialysis. Don't sell my bed, though. I'll be back next semester."

I hung up the phone slowly and stared at his vacant bed. Our room seemed empty without him, and I felt as if I'd lost my left arm. Part of me went missing when Mark left.

In true Mark Burrell fashion, however, he remained optimistic. "Don't worry, Ken Brown. I'll be back next semester."

But next semester never came.

After he lost one of his kidneys, I went home to visit him. I shuddered when I saw him hooked up to the dialysis equipment. Together, we had looked forward to the future, and now he was back in Chicago and chained to a box.

He'd lost a lot of weight. "Hey, for the first time in my life, I'm skinny. I've got nothing to complain about."

A year later, Mark received a kidney transplant. But he never returned to SIU. Instead, he enrolled at Chicago State University to be near his home.

His new kidney gave him fifteen good years.

chapter fifteen

"When You Graduate, You Have a Job"

"He that tilleth his land shall have plenty
of bread: but he that followeth after vain persons
shall have poverty enough."
— Proverbs 28:19

One day during my second year, I walked into The Saluki Grill to meet Deidre for lunch. The Saluki was a small café located in the basement of the cafeteria building. Our room and board fees covered the cost of cafeteria food, but if you missed the cafeteria hours, or simply wanted a change of pace, you could eat some fast food or a snack at The Saluki. It also had arcade game machines, which made it a popular hangout.

Deidre hadn't arrived, so while I waited, I played a couple games of Pac Man. In between games, I glanced at the man working in the kitchen—the activity in a commercial kitchen often attracted my attention. I'd seen that man there many times before. In the past, a student worker assisted him, but lately he worked alone. He had rosy cheeks and a salt-and-pepper beard; he looked to be in his mid-forties. He scurried around, flipping burgers and trying to wash dishes at the same time.

To this day, I'm not sure exactly what came over me—another impulsive act, I guess. I left the video game and walked over to the counter. "Excuse me, sir. You looking for help?" I had no plans to ask for a job when I walked in there.

He looked up at me and wiped his hands on his white apron. "Matter of fact, I am."

"Well, I'm a food and nutrition major, and I'd be glad to work for you."

Two days later, I started the job that began my food services career. I smiled when I put on the maroon apron that read The Saluki Grill across the chest. I immediately felt comfortable working at the grill—and for the owner, Jack Beard.

Jack methodically taught me the business. First, he put me in charge of running the cash register and servicing our customers. When I mastered those jobs, he let me cook. He showed me how to make the Saluki Burger, which was a large burger made from two patties and Jack's special sauce. It was a lot like a Big Mac. I also fried the French fries, grilled the cheese sandwiches, and assembled the Cobb salads.

I looked forward to going to work every day. People like Dad, Twitch, and my fraternity brothers had instilled in me a passion for excellence, and I tried to approach my job in a way that would make them proud. I made sure the café was always sparkling clean; I never served sub-par food; and I smiled and talked to the customers. What I had always felt in my gut, I found to be true—I loved the business of food and service.

After I tackled the cooking jobs, Jack taught me the finer points of running the overall business. At the end of one day, he motioned me into the back office. The money drawer from the register sat on the desk.

"Come here. I want to show you how to count down the drawer." He demonstrated how to count and organize the money, reconcile it to the receipt report, record the discounted meals, and prepare the drawer for the following day. "Now, Ken. It's only you and me with this drawer. I don't want no silent partners."

"Yes, sir."

Then he explained the back office operation: how to order food, manage the receipts, inventory the stock, and keep the books. Jack was patient and methodical as he taught me. The knowledge he shared fed my passion. The more he taught me, the more I wanted to learn.

"Look, Ken. I like you. You work hard, and you're respectful. I'm starting another business, and I need a student manager to close the grill every day. You interested?"

"You bet!"

"I'll raise your pay to $5.85 an hour." Then he reached into his pocket, pulled out a set of keys, and tossed them to me.

"You've learned a lot. You'll be a great manager."

I appreciated the increase in pay, but what really felt good was the moment I caught those keys. "Thanks for your trust. I won't let you down."

Jack was an entrepreneur at heart. A few weeks later, he told me that he'd bought some land to develop. "Students don't have enough housing options around here. I'm going to develop a nice mobile home park as an alternative to the dorms."

Over the next eight months, Jack shared the detailed plans for his development. After he completed it, and students filled it up, he didn't rest long. "Now those kids need some place to do their laundry." So he opened a laundromat near the park. Jack was a visionary, a risk-taker, but he also possessed the organizational skills to see something to fruition.

I worked at The Saluki Grill for two years. But as I entered my senior year and approached graduation, I thought about getting some additional experience. My guidance counselor was a petite Korean woman by the name of Dr. Ashraf. She was easy to talk with and was always interested in our progress toward getting a job.

"You have to have practical experience by the time you graduate," she told the students in the Food and Nutrition Department. "You won't get hired just because you have good grades. You have to bring value to the job."

To encourage us in pursuing real world experience, she arranged internships with various organizations. She'd visit our classes and announce different opportunities: "A friend of mine at a hotel is looking for an intern. Anyone interested?" "Thoreau's Restaurant is looking for someone to wait tables." "The Student Union is looking for an intern."

She also urged us to work hard on writing our résumés. "A good résumé will get you in the door."

I knew my job as a Student Manager would look good on my résumé. But I still kept my ears out for other opportunities.

One day, Dr. Ashraf came to my class. "The Marriott Corporation is seeking interns in their food services operation here on campus," she said.

Marriott! That'd look great on my résumé.

The Marriott Corporation owned the contract on all the food service operations for SIU. They handled the cafeterias, as well as special catering events for the administration and visiting dignitaries.

I interviewed for one of the intern positions and got the job. On my first day, the Food Services Director, Ms. Token, gave me a tour of the huge on-campus kitchen facility. I walked around and gazed at the stainless steel ovens, grills, and prep tables. Everything was clean and organized. The place reminded me of the kitchens where Dad and Grandma had worked.

Each day, Ms. Token met with the other interns and me and assigned us our tasks. We provided Marriott with cheap labor, but in return, they taught us the business. One day they'd assign me to work on a banquet room setup, where I learned to roll the white linen napkins and properly arrange the formal dinnerware. Another day, I'd wait tables. Or I'd work on the cafeteria line or help prepare a catered meal. Later, I learned their processes for inventory control, procurement, vendor management, and managing the budget.

The Marriott also taught me their perspective on excellence. "Well-prepared food is only half the equation," Ms. Token said. "An excellent presentation is the other half. The customer must feel good about the whole dining experience."

Dignitaries often visited SIU—such as Governor James Thompson or Senator Paul Simon—and the university president would hold a formal luncheon in their honor. The Marriott ran those luncheons, and the presentation of the food and the dining hall was always top-notch.

During my internship, I observed Ms. Token and the rest of the staff. I studied how they interacted with others and how they approached their individual jobs, and I visualized myself doing Ms. Token's job—organizing, delegating, and overseeing.

That's what I want to do.

After the internship concluded, I drafted my résumé. In large bold letters, I included the words: "MARRIOTT CORPORATION" and "STUDENT MANAGER."

As the spring of my senior year approached, I focused on finding a permanent job after graduation. Earning a diploma wasn't my goal—landing a respectable job was. I never forgot the naysayers' doubts about the value of college. I can't stand the thought of returning home without a respectable job.

Several times a week, I passed through the administration building, Woody Hall, and inspected the company postings for job interviews. I looked during February but didn't see anything relevant to my major. Nothing showed up in March, either. During the beginning of April, however, I glanced over the postings and spotted one from Aramark— a food services company like Marriott. It read: "Aramark is seeking interviews with qualified candidates for an entry-level management position. A bachelor's degree in Food and Nutrition is required. Experience is a plus. Job placement will be in the Chicago area."

I'm all over this! I've got the education, the experience, and I can go home with a great job in hand. I signed up for an interview and picked the first time slot: two weeks later at eight o'clock in the morning. This is the culmination of everything I've worked for.

I spoke with Richard Gardner from my fraternity, and he gave me pointers on interviewing: "Research the company beforehand." "Look the interviewer in the eye." "Know your answers to the most likely questions."

And then I talked to Shawn Moore about interview clothes. "Dress to impress" was one of the mottoes of our fraternity, and Shawn was probably the best-dressed brother in our chapter. "Polish your shoes. People look at your shoes first," he said. "I'll help you find a stylish suit. You'll need a pocket-handkerchief and a red power tie. Make sure your dress shirt is crisp with no yellow around the collar."

On Monday morning at 7:30, I grabbed my briefcase (which contained nothing but three copies of my résumé) and headed over to Woody Hall. I walked with nervous energy. It rained hard, and I kept under my umbrella to avoid getting my blue suit wet.

I arrived at Woody Hall before my interviewer, so I sat on a chair outside the interview room. It was 7:45.

Fifteen minutes passed and no one showed up.

My knees bounced as I stared at the outside door and waited.

Fifteen more minutes passed. No one.

I've messed up! I've probably come at the wrong time. Did I miss my interview?

My stomach churned and sweat dripped from my forehead.

Finally at 8:25, the door swung open, and a man wearing a gray trench coat charged in. Water dripped off his hat and briefcase.

He strode over to me, breathing heavily. "I'm so sorry I'm late," he said with a scratchy smoker's voice. He shook my hand. "I got stuck in traffic. I can't apologize enough. It's terribly rude for me to have kept you waiting like this."

I'd pictured my interviewer as a young man with slicked-back hair who would pound me with tough questions. But this man was older, relaxed, and so apologetic, that he put me at ease.

"My name's Rick Weber. It's a pleasure to meet you." Water dripped from his hair to his collar, and he reached back to wipe it off. "Again, please accept my apologies."

"It's no problem at all, Mr. Weber."

Something about his polite manners and less-than-graceful entrance boosted my confidence. I'm in control here. All I have to do is be myself.

"I see you're from Chicago," he said. "I am, too."

His questions were easy. Basically, he wanted to hear me speak: "Tell me about yourself." "What are your strengths and weaknesses?" "What are you passionate about?"

That last question opened the door for me. "Serving people with excellence," I began. I talked so fast, I had to slow myself down so he could understand me. I told him about my family history and the values my parents instilled in me. I told him about The Saluki Grill and how Jack witnessed my work ethic and trusted me to be a manager. And I told him about the lessons on excellence I learned from Marriott.

Mr. Weber suddenly looked at his watch and stood up. He extended his hand to me. "Mr. Brown. I've heard all I need to hear."

Oh, no.

"When you graduate, you have a job."

"What?"

"We'll assign you as an Assistant Food Services Director in the Chicago area."

I walked out of Woody Hall, closed the door, and pumped my fist into the air. "Yes!" I went straight to Deidre's room and told her. She hugged me and cried with joy. Then I told my fraternity brothers. "You've made the big time," Richard said. "We're proud of you."

A week later, I received a letter from Mr. Weber. "Dear Mr. Brown," it said. "We're excited to welcome you on board at Aramark. You'll be assigned to our food services operation at

National Lewis University in Evanston, Illinois. Your starting salary will be $18,000 per year."

"Woo! Eighteen thousand!" I couldn't believe it. What am I going to do with that much money?

I raced to my phone and called my mom. "Guess what, Mu'dear? I got a job. I'm coming home."

PART 2 — CAREER PATH OF OBEDIENCE

chapter sixteen

A Different Kind of Eviction

"It takes both rain and sunshine to
make a rainbow." — Unknown

After college, I returned to Chicago and moved into Granny's one-bedroom apartment. Granny kept strange sleeping habits—she never slept in her room but just napped on her sofa—so I got to use her room. I planned to live with her for six months, save my money, and then get my own place.

On my first day of work, I put on my suit, grabbed my briefcase, and hopped the 8:30 train to Evanston. It was a two-hour ride. I fidgeted as I rode along with the other professionals on their way to work. *This is for real. I'm a working man now!*

I arrived at Lewis University and found the Aramark offices in the back of the cafeteria building. Like Marriott at SIU, Aramark owned the food services contract on campus—specifically, the cafeteria operation, as well as special banquets and catering jobs. I opened the double glass doors and entered the office; my heart pounded hard against my chest.

A woman came up and introduced herself. "Hello. My name's Mary." She was Caucasian, probably in her mid-twenties. She wore brown corduroy pants and a tan turtleneck sweater, and her brown hair was pulled back tight behind her head. "I'm the director here, and you'll be reporting to me. I just started last week."

Mary took me on a tour of the office and kitchen and introduced me to the staff. "Rick told me great things about you. Said you have a real personable style." Mary looked at me and frowned. "Let me tell you something about my style. I'm the director, so I'm in charge. I'll deal with the president and the department heads. I believe in formal lines of authority. Are we clear?"

"Yes, ma'am."

"I'll let you manage the people and take care of acquiring the food and supplies."

Mary led me to two private offices in the back. The one on the right was hers. She pointed to the one on the left. "This office is yours. I'll give you a few minutes to get set up."

I stepped inside. On the desk sat a nameplate that read: "Ken Brown, Assistant Director." I ran my finger along the engraved lettering. *Nice.*

Opening my briefcase, I pulled out photographs of Deidre and my family and arranged them on the desk. Next to them, I placed a paperweight that my fraternity brothers gave me when I left SIU. It had an imprint of the Alpha Phi Alpha logo—a black and gold shield. I sat in the rolling desk chair and rested my hands on top of the desk. *This is sweet. Look at me—Kenny from the block.*

I spun around in the chair and smiled. *I'm set. This is a huge company. I can work for them forever.* After a few minutes, I went over to Mary in her office. "I'm ready. Show me where to begin."

The job suited me perfectly. My management experience from The Saluki Grill and customer service knowledge from Marriott came in handy as I acclimated myself. During my first few months, Deidre worked as a student teacher in Murphysboro, so I didn't get to see her much at all. That gave me time to focus on my job. On a few weekends, I visited her and took her out to nice restaurants. We enjoyed having a little money to spend.

As the assistant director, I ensured that the meals were prepared well and on time, developed the menu, ordered the food, and rented the equipment when we held large banquets. I was only twenty-two when I started, and the average age of the staff was probably forty. But I wasn't intimidated. I loved people, and I enjoyed talking with them.

The staff supervisor, Jonnie, reported directly to me. She was a large black lady with a short Afro. She'd been born and raised in Evanston, and she knew the college president personally. "I've been here since the beginning," she told me. "I know how to run things." She managed the cooks and other workers, counted down the drawers after each meal, and balanced the accounting books.

Other people in my position might've taken a firm approach with Jonnie to establish authority, but that wasn't my style. At The Saluki Grill, Jack Beard trusted me to do my job well, and I helped him accomplish his goals. My job objectives could be achieved through Jonnie, so I befriended her. We talked often and laughed. I let her do her job, and she did it well.

However, I was still a hands-on manager. I dressed sharp, but I took off my jacket, rolled up my sleeves, and mingled with the cooks and students. Sometimes, I jumped in the prep line and rolled burritos, or I might clean the tables or refill the salad bar. I talked with everyone: the cooks, the dishwasher, and the students.

I spoke often with the students to see how we were doing. "How was the food tonight?" I asked the kids. "What can we do differently?"

"The weekly menus rarely change," several students said.

I called Deidre who was working near SIU and asked her to grab some of their menus. I copied what they did and added my own flair. We put on Spanish Night once a month, and I adorned the room with piñatas and other Latin American decorations. We instituted other theme meals like Italian Night and Breakfast-for-Dinner.

"The food's finally interesting around here," said one student.

"I look forward to coming to the cafeteria now," said another.

When the school held special banquets, I remembered my Marriott training: presentation is half of the dining experience. I ordered linen napkins and arranged the place settings in an elegant manner. I added extra touches like garnishes to the entrees and pretty sauces to the desserts. As people finished their meals, I sauntered around the ballroom and asked the attendees how they liked the meal.

After one banquet, the president, Orly Roberts, came back to our office. He was a large man, but very approachable. He stopped outside Mary's office.

"Hello, Mr. President," I heard Mary say.

"I just wanted to thank you for the great food at the banquet," Mr. Roberts said. "It was excellent."

He then turned and looked at me in my office. "I've

been watching you, Ken. You're very professional. You've done a great job these past few months."

I smiled. "Thank you, sir."

Mary never gave me feedback, but I was okay with that; I knew I was doing a good job. But it sure felt good for the president to stop in and tell me that. He often left me notes after other banquets: "Ken, great job today. Thank you."

Mary worked from seven in the morning until three in the afternoon. I arrived at eleven every morning and stayed until after we closed at seven. Some evenings after we closed, I'd sit at my desk and ponder the future. I visualized working Mary's job as a director and even Rick Weber's job as a regional director over multiple campuses. *Aramark can keep me growing and learning for a long time.*

Late one afternoon, about three months into my job, Mr. Roberts walked into the office. His forehead was furrowed, and he looked troubled. Jonnie was still in the kitchen, and Mary had gone home.

"Ken," he said. "I've got a problem, and I was wondering if you could help."

"Yes, sir. Anything."

"Michael Lewis's private cook walked out on him today, and I need to find him someone. You know anyone?"

Michael Lewis was a wealthy man who lived in a mansion across the street from the campus. He was the school's largest donor, and a few years before, the school changed its name from National University to Lewis University in honor of his generosity.

At first, I thought Mr. Roberts wanted someone to

prepare Mr. Lewis's dinner that evening. "I can send over one of our cooks."

"No. We've ordered something for him tonight. I need a permanent replacement. Do you know any good cooks?"

"Do I ever. My mother and grandmother are incredible cooks."

"Oh, really? Can you get them up here tomorrow?"

As soon as he left, I grabbed the phone and called my mom. "Mu'dear, you won't believe the job I've got for you."

Mu'dear and Granny drove to Evanston the next day and met with Mr. Lewis at his home. Afterward, Mu'dear and Granny stopped by my office; it was the first time they'd seen it. They both smiled as if they'd won a million dollars.

"Look at you," Granny said, picking up the nameplate from my desk. "Ken Brown. Assistant Director. You've made it big."

"I always knew he would," Mu'dear said.

It felt good to make them proud, but I was dying to know what Mr. Lewis had said.

"He hired us both!" Mu'dear said. "We'll rotate working four days at a time and we'll live at his house when we're there. We'll have our own apartment in a wing of the estate."

"That's awesome!"

"Wait. This is the best part. He's going to pay us, each, $600 per week."

"No way!" They would make more money than I did. After everything Mu'dear had been through, she would make $30,000 a year and live part-time in a mansion.

Things were moving along beautifully. Granny and Mu'dear now worked nearby. And I loved my job. I felt at home.

One Friday in March, Mary stopped in my office before heading home. "I need to switch schedules with you on Monday. Can you open?"

"Sure. No problem."

Mary partied a lot, and I figured she had a late night party to attend on Sunday. I didn't mind. I could be home by five o'clock and enjoy a rare evening to relax. But on Monday morning, I learned that a party had nothing to do with the schedule change.

As soon as I walked through the double glass doors at 6:45, Mary poked her head out of her office. "Ken, let's talk. Come in here please."

What's she doing here? I stepped into her office.

"Take a seat," she said without even saying hello.

Something's not right.

She seemed to look through me; her face showed no emotion. "You know, Ken, our management styles are very different."

"Yeah, I know. We complement each other. I think it's great."

"No. It's not great." She cleared her throat. "I've got to let you go."

"Go? Where am I going?"

I tried to figure out what she was talking about. *Maybe Rick's transferring me closer to home.*

"It's not working out. I've got to terminate you."

I squinted at her. It took several seconds for her words to sink in. "Terminate?" I said slowly. "You're firing me?"

"Yes. I need you to clean out your office."

I had received no reprimands. No warnings. No

nothing. I simply couldn't believe what she was saying. *This is wrong.* Shock and anger overcame me, and my emotions took over. "You're out of your mind! You can't let me go. You didn't hire me; you can't fire me."

"Listen, Ken. Don't make this worse than it already is. I'm the director, and I say you're fired."

I felt like a judge had evicted me once again. My eyes stung, and only my anger kept me from crying. "You can't do this. I want to talk to Rick. I can be transferred. This is a big company."

"You're assigned to me, and it's my decision."

My muscles tightened. I balled my hands into fists. I glanced around the room, as if answers lay hidden in some corner. "I'm not going anywhere. I want to see my file." I didn't know what I wanted to look for in my file—just anything to make sense of what she was doing.

Mary pulled it from her cabinet drawer and dropped it on the desk.

I leafed through it, but there was nothing there except routine administrative paperwork.

"Now clean out your office."

"No. I want to talk to Rick. He recruited me, and he didn't recruit me for no six months. I could've worked somewhere else. You all playing some type of game with me?"

She sat stone-faced and slid the phone toward me. It had a speed-dial button labeled: "Rick Weber."

I pressed the button. "I need to speak with Mr. Weber."

"I'm sorry," his secretary said. "He's on vacation for the next two weeks. Can I take a message?"

I didn't know what to do. "No, thank you," I said and

hung up.

I glared at her. *You planned this. You waited until Rick went on vacation. You malicious witch.* I didn't want to leave; I wanted to fight.

But she had me.

We sat silently for what seemed like several minutes. In some strange way, I felt if I refused to leave, I could avoid the reality of what was happening.

Then Mary stood up. "You need to leave now," she said and walked out.

Having no choice, I slowly reached for my briefcase and staggered into my office. My legs felt numb. *I've done great work. I've come in early. Stayed late. I've got a great rapport with the staff, and Mr. Roberts likes my work.*

I shook my head. "What have I done?"

I thought of Deidre and Mu'dear and my fraternity brothers. *What will they think? They've been so proud of me.*

Summoning my willpower not to cry, I picked up an empty cardboard potato chip box and filled it with my belongings: my files, photographs, fraternity paperweight, and my nameplate—assistant director no longer. I threw my key on the desk and snuck out the back exit.

I didn't say good-bye to anyone—even Jonnie. *What would she think of me?*

I descended the concrete stairs and left through the loading dock—a deliveryman unloaded a shipment of frozen meats, and I stepped around him. Stopping at the end of the dock, I gazed at the nearby street, but I couldn't focus my eyes. My body trembled.

As a thirteen-year-old, I carried my bag of clothes from place to place, and now, I carried my box of office belongings in the same way. But during the evictions, I had my family with me. Now I was alone.

What am I going to do?

chapter seventeen

SIXTY DAYS
OF SORROW

"Defeat never comes to any man until he admits it."
— Joseph Daniels

I stood on the loading dock for several minutes not knowing which way to turn. *I can't believe this is happening.*

Looking across the street, I gazed at Mr. Lewis's mansion. *Mu'dear might be there.* Mr. Lewis had gone to his winter villa in Arizona and taken Granny with him, but Mu'dear still stopped by his house to walk the dogs and take in the mail.

The tears started as soon as I crossed the street. Like a sudden thunderstorm, they flooded my eyes so I could barely see. I tried to look for oncoming traffic, but I was too distraught to really care.

At the house, I rang the doorbell. Mu'dear answered. I set down my box, and buried my face in her shoulder. I cried so hard that I nearly hyperventilated. Sobbing against her shoulder, I could taste the fabric of her sweater. I tried to talk, but all I could get out were erratic sounds.

"What's wrong with you, boy?" She wrapped her arms around me. "What's wrong with you?"

I couldn't talk. I was as out of control as my world.

"Speak to me. What's going on?" She patted my back.

"She..." I breathed in spasms. "She..."

"Okay. Shhh," she said. "Just relax." Her arms tightened, and after a minute or two, I calmed down. "Who is *she*? Tell me what happened."

"I got fired, Mu'dear. She fired me. Mary fired me."

"What?" Mu'dear shouted insults, calling Mary more bad words than I thought she knew. "She's jealous," Mu'dear added. "She can't hold a candle to you, and she knows it. She's inept. Worthless. She's afraid you'll take her job."

Mu'dear's words were hurled in hatred, but it felt good to hear them.

"I'm going right over there," she said. "I'm going to have a word with that little tramp."

"No, Mu'dear," I said, straightening up. "No, you're not." I appreciated her defense, but I couldn't let her fight my battles. I wasn't a kid anymore, and I had enough embarrassment to deal with. "It's not your fight. I don't want no one to have anything to do with her."

I let go of her. "I gotta go. Thanks, Mu'dear." I picked up my belongings. "I'll be okay," I muttered.

"I'll call you tonight," she said as I walked away. "Everything will work out."

I caught the train to Granny's apartment. I was glad Granny wouldn't be home; I wanted to be alone and hide. Holding my box in my lap, I rested my head against the window and let the tears fall. A man sitting catty-corner across the aisle stared at me but said nothing. Countless questions raced through my mind. *Did I say something wrong? What has she said about me? What do I tell people? How do I find another job?*

My parents had promised good things would happen if I gave one hundred percent. "If you work hard and achieve excellence, you'll be rewarded," Mu'dear said. I had believed in the faith of my mother and now that faith had proven worthless. *I strove for excellence, and it got me fired.*

After the long ride, I arrived at the stop for Granny's apartment. I disembarked and squeezed through the crowd of people boarding the train on their way to work. It was nine o'clock.

I entered Granny's apartment, locked the door behind me, and collapsed into bed. For the rest of the morning, I cried periodically. I heard a phone ring in the distance. I knew it was mine, but I made no effort to get up and answer it. Sometime later, I woke long enough to read the digital clock—two o'clock. I hadn't eaten all day; I felt sick to my stomach. The last thing I wanted was food.

The doorbell rang, but I was like a rock—unable to move. Whoever it was, rang again, then finally left. By three o'clock, my tears had dried, and I lay on my back gazing at the ceiling. *Lord, why is this happening? What did I do to deserve this?* But I heard no answer—only the sounds of passing cars nine stories below, where the world went about its business without me.

By five o'clock, the sunlight seeping through Granny's yellow curtains began to fade. Later, the phone rang again, and then rang almost every ten minutes for the next two hours. Darkness swallowed the room. And with the darkness came more tears. In agony, I bit my pillow as hard as I could. As eight o'clock passed, I heard an ambulance approach my building. If only it'd come and take me away. I didn't care where—just far enough so I could hide and suffer no more embarrassment.

At nine, the outside sounds quieted and were replaced by the constant dripping of the bathroom faucet. I rolled over, away from the bathroom, and muffled the dripping sound with the other pillow.

After ten sometime, I shot up in bed. I'd fallen asleep and dreamed I was standing outside my house on South Bishop. All my belongings sat piled on the sidewalk. I watched helplessly as my neighbor Jerome rifled through my stuff, taking whatever he wanted. I stood there, my feet frozen to the pavement. "No!" I yelled, but Jerome didn't hear me.

I tossed and turned for three hours before falling back asleep. But a restless dream woke me up again. The clock read two o'clock. I lay on my stomach for a while, then my left side, my back, and my right side. And then back to my stomach again. I stayed awake. The inside corner of my eyes burned, and it hurt to touch them.

Four agonizing hours later, light sifted through the curtains and the sounds of the street returned to life.

The phone rang. I dragged myself from bed, staggered to the kitchen, and listened to the answering machine as my mother spoke. I picked up the phone. "Hi, Mu'dear. I'm okay, but I don't want to talk right now."

Before I returned to bed, Deidre called; she'd heard what happened.

"I'm sorry, Dee. I just don't have it in me to talk. I don't have any energy." My face burned with embarrassment as I spoke.

"Everything's going to be okay, Kenny."

"I gotta go."

For two weeks, I stayed in bed, shifting between periods of fitful naps, complete numbness, and tormented questioning. A few times a day, I got up to use the bathroom and eat crackers in the kitchen. While up, I'd check the answering machine. Most of the calls were from family or Deidre, but one day, I received a message from Mary. "Please call me," she said.

Fat chance.

For days, I didn't shower. I didn't open the curtains. I didn't turn on the television or the radio. Mu'dear, Granny, and Deidre called each day, but for the most part, I didn't want to talk. *I just want to disappear.*

Then two weeks after my firing, the phone rang and this time, for some reason, I didn't screen the call. It was Mary again. "Ken, could you please call Orly Roberts?"

"For what?" I said through gritted teeth.

"He's really concerned about your termination. Please tell him that it's Aramark business."

I can't believe the nerve of you, lady. I didn't say anything. I just held the phone to my ear and stared at the kitchen table.

"Ken? Are you there? Can you call Mr. Roberts?"

"No. I can't." I slammed down the phone and stormed back into the bedroom. But instead of falling back into bed, I paced around the room. How dare she! I went to the window and tore open the curtains.

Lake Michigan glistened in the afternoon sun. "She can go to hell!"

I stared out the window for about half an hour and cursed Mary. And then, for the first time in fourteen days, I went in the bathroom and took a shower. The anger I felt after Mary's call changed something in me. I no longer wanted to crawl back in bed.

When I came out of the shower, the phone rang again, and I answered it. It was Mu'dear. We talked for about an hour, and as we talked, I felt a familiar comfort like a hug come over me—the comfort I felt growing up when Mu'dear forced me to talk about my troubles. By the end of those childhood conversations, we joked and laughed. I wasn't laughing, now. But I appreciated the call.

Before we hung up, Mu'dear promised she'd call the next day.

"That'd be fine," I said, and I meant it. I looked forward to her calling back.

She called me every day for the next two months, and we rarely spoke for less than an hour. During that time, I opened the curtains in the apartment every morning. I still sulked, but for the most part, I stayed out of bed until nighttime.

Granny phoned from Arizona and told me not to worry about expenses. "You helped me when you were working. Now it's my turn. I'll make sure the bills get paid."

Other friends called to cheer me up. Several of them urged me to take legal action against Aramark. "If there was no cause for your firing, then it was racism. You need to sue."

Another friend encouraged me to call the NAACP. "Don't take this sitting down."

"Maybe that's the answer," I said. "I'll think about it."

For several weeks, I considered filing a lawsuit. I didn't know what else to do. I couldn't envision how my life was going to move forward. I didn't know how I'd get another job, and I figured whatever I found would be an embarrassment. *I'll end up with some maintenance job, and it'll prove the college naysayers right.*

I might've pursued legal action, if not for one person—Deidre. After those first two weeks, Deidre came over often. She encouraged me. "You have a lot going for you. You'll find another job, and it'll be even better than Aramark."

She listened to me. Even when I refused to believe her optimism, she sat quietly and let me have my say. Sometimes, she came over and we hardly talked at all. We'd sit on the sofa and watch television. I'd lean against her, and we'd rest our heads together. I'd smell her skin and feel her hair against my cheek. She gave me peace.

A month later, Deidre persuaded me to leave the apartment. After scraping together five dollars, we rode the elevator to the first floor and got takeout from the Chinese restaurant. We grabbed a box of rice, some egg rolls, and two Pepsi's, and returned to the apartment to watch a movie that Deidre had brought. We did that, off and on, for the next several weeks.

As the two-month anniversary of my dismissal approached, I felt myself coming back to life. Talking to Mu'dear—as it was for many people—was good therapy. Plus, I couldn't look at Deidre and experience her love and support and still see my life as hopeless.

"I'm not going to sue Aramark," I told Deidre. "I just want to put them in the past. It'll take too much energy—negative energy. I don't want to stoop to that level."

My fraternity brother Shawn Moore also called me from time to time. He was looking for a new job, and he called me after his interviews. "You need to start looking, too."

In two months, I never even opened up the newspaper want ads. I didn't want to live off Granny, but I felt frozen—just like Mu'dear must've felt when the judge ordered our eviction from South Bishop. *How do I move forward?*

But one night Shawn called me. "What're you doing tomorrow?"

"Nothing."

"I'm going to a minority job fair. You wanna come?"

I looked out the family room window and gazed at the moon hovering over the lake. *It would be nice to get outside again.* "Why not? Let's go."

I slept peacefully that night, even though I didn't expect much from the fair. I didn't expect a job. And I certainly didn't expect a job that was bigger and better than the one at Aramark.

chapter eighteen

Back Among the Living

"We conquer not in any brilliant fashion, we conquer by continuing." — George Matheson

S hawn stopped by my apartment in the morning, and we walked to the train station. It was a sunny June day, and I breathed in the fresh smells around me. We entered the station and as I pushed through the turnstile, I smiled. *It's good to be among the living again.*

The job fair was held in a large banquet hall on the campus of DePaul University. For a few minutes, I stood outside the room and gazed inside. One hundred or more companies had set up booths throughout the room. Banners hung from the high walls, and the booths were decorated with large company logos as well as balloons and streamers. People scurried along the grid of walkways to distribute their résumés and talk with company recruiters.

Dr. Ashraf and my fraternity brothers had taught me to avoid discussing bad experiences when interviewing for a job. So, I left my experience at Aramark off my résumé. It was like that time never existed. *What do I say about the last nine months? Surely, nobody's gonna hire me if I can't show work since graduation.*

But despite my low confidence, I took a deep breath and walked into the room. Shawn was interested in a sales position, and he wanted to talk with everyone. "I'm just interested in food," I said. "I'd like to find another assistant director position." We agreed to separate and meet up later.

I sauntered down the first aisle, looking for hotel or food services companies like Marriott or Hyatt. I spotted companies like IBM, Honeywell, and 3M, but nothing in my field. As I walked down the fourth aisle, I approached a booth for Ponderosa Restaurants. *Not exactly what I'm looking for, but it is food.*

I stopped and spoke with them for a few minutes. A man told me about the company and asked for my résumé. He looked it over and, in a monotonous voice, said he'd call if he had any openings. I walked on.

In the next aisle, I drew near a booth for the Wendy's fast food chain. They had one of the biggest booths at the fair. On the back wall hung the large Wendy's logo with the red-haired girl, and blue ribbons dangled from the sides of the booth. *Nah, I don't want to do fast food. I've got a college degree. I could've stayed home if I wanted to flip burgers.*

Unlike the representatives at other booths, the Wendy's recruiters ventured into the aisle and shook hands with people as they came by. A woman approached me and smiled. She was dressed in a blue tailored suit. "Hi, I'm Jennifer with Wendy's International."

"International?"

"Yes, Wendy's is a multi-national corporation. We have almost four thousand restaurants located all over the world."

She went on to explain the corporate structure and their management program. "We're looking for qualified people to come in as manager trainees. Once trained, they'll move into manager positions and, later, general manager positions over multiple stores."

I hadn't thought of fast food as anything more than what I observed behind a McDonald's counter. *It can't hurt to talk to them.*

Jennifer asked to see my résumé, and she looked it over. "Would you mind coming over to the booth for a minute?"

I followed her to the booth, where she caught the attention of another Wendy's recruiter.

"Look at this," she told the man as she handed him the résumé.

My stomach tingled, and I remembered the way I'd felt when I interviewed with Rick Weber. *It's nice to impress somebody again. But don't get your hopes up yet.*

The man studied my background and invited me to come behind a black curtain for an impromptu interview. I hadn't prepared to answer interview questions, but fortunately my Aramark interview was fresh in my mind, and I drew on that experience to demonstrate the same passion for excellence.

When we finished, the man shook my hand and smiled. "Thank you for your time. We'll be in touch soon."

A few days later, a man from Wendy's called and requested that I come to their regional headquarters for some follow-up interviews. I went, and the conversations seemed to go well—talking always came easily to me.

For the next week, nervous energy coursed through my body. I woke before the alarm each morning, and I could barely sit still during the day. Two months before, I couldn't drag myself out of bed. Now I couldn't stop fidgeting. I took walks by the lake, or I paced around the kitchen while talking on the phone. Every time the phone rang, I ran to it, thinking it might be someone from Wendy's.

Finally, I received a letter in the mail. It was from Wendy's International, and it read: "Congratulations. We are pleased to make you an offer as a manager trainee. Your assignment will be in downtown Chicago, at the Clark and Madison store. You will report to the general manager, Mark Ghee. Your starting salary will be $18,500 per year."

"All right! I even got a raise!"

I immediately called Deidre, Mu'dear, and Shawn to tell them the great news. *So this is what life is like after Mary. It's not bad at all. I'm back!*

As I crossed the street in front of the Clark and Madison Wendy's, I passed an Aramark laundry services truck parked along the curb. I felt a flush of embarrassment, took a deep breath, and continued into the restaurant. I was immediately confronted with a bustle of activity.

The store was in the heart of downtown Chicago, across the street from the First National Bank building. It covered three floors. Plush carpeting and pendulum lighting decorated the dining room. A hostess greeted me and directed me to one of the four counters.

I told her I was there to meet Mark Ghee. A few minutes later, a tall man with red hair and a thick mustache came out and shook my hand.

"It's a pleasure to have you with us, Ken. I've heard great things about you."

"I'm excited to be here."

"Great. Because you're going to learn a lot. I'm going to teach you everything I know." He put his hand on my shoulder and smiled. "You'll stay in the training program for about six weeks, and if everything goes well—and I know it will—you'll be promoted to manager. Just remember, the most important word around here is quality—quality of food and quality of service."

I quickly learned that Mark didn't throw around empty slogans. When he said that quality was our most important focus, he meant it.

Mark was a leader and a coach, and he treated every day at the restaurant like a sports game. Before each shift, he huddled the managers together and reviewed our targets for sales and service times. Occasionally, he mentioned a company contest for stores in our region. The contests were often based on things like sales of a particular new item, total sales, or average customer transaction time.

"We're going to win this contest," Mark would say. "Although the prize money goes to the general manager, I'm going to share it evenly with you all."

Then at the end of a pre-shift meeting, he'd say, "We've got the best team in the company. Now let's go out there and show them how it's done."

For six weeks, Mark walked me through the systems involved in running the business. There were detailed, documented processes for cooking everything: hamburgers, fries, baked potatoes, chili—as well as for maintaining and cleaning the restaurant. "Experience has proven that these systems work," he said. "We ensure the quality of our product by adhering to them."

Mark often paced around the kitchen with a stopwatch.

We were supposed to prepare and present every customer's order in less than sixty seconds. During one of the first times I managed a crew, the service times ran slower than normal. Mark put his hand on my shoulder. "Can you come back to the office for a second?"

I went back, and once we were out of earshot of everyone else, Mark informed me that our times were too slow. He explained how to correct the situation. "I believe in you. You're doing a great job." He patted me on the back. "Now let's work on doing even better."

And I did do better. I wanted to succeed because of Mark—I wanted to please him.

As I mastered the operations side of things, Mark taught me about the back office. He showed me the financial statements and explained how to manage expenses and capital improvements, and how to measure profit. Work each day was like playing in a ten-hour basketball game, but I rarely went home tired. The busyness of the job stimulated me, and Mark's motivating nature made it fun.

After my first six weeks, Mark gathered the managers around him. "I'd like to congratulate Ken on his promotion to manager." He looked at me and clapped. The others clapped along. "You've performed extremely well. I'm proud of you."

Mark was a family man—his office was filled with pictures of his wife and kids. And he was a gentleman. I never witnessed him reprimand someone in public; he always pulled them aside to a private spot and spoke to them in a quiet tone. But when he rewarded somebody, like for winning an in-store contest, he'd make a big deal out of it. He made sure all the employees knew of the person's accomplishment. Regardless of how busy we got, he maintained his cool and ran the restaurant like clockwork.

His style was quite different than what I experienced at Aramark. Mark educated and delegated. Mary had coveted certain responsibilities, and she wouldn't teach me what she did. When my relationship with Orly Roberts or my family's relationship with Michael Lewis threatened her, she fired me. I'd wanted to climb up the Aramark corporate ladder, but God had different plans for me. Like Judas in the Bible, Mary played an important role in my life—I would've never learned from people like Mark Ghee if I'd spent my career at Aramark.

The evictions and job termination, I believe, were God's way of keeping me from getting too comfortable. Future events would surely yank me from my settled path, and I would need to be ready to experience and learn new things.

I worked for Mark Ghee for one year. I still consider him to be the best leader I've ever reported to. "Leadership isn't about you," he said. "It's about the seeds you plant. If you're a good leader, you can leave a situation and it won't change. The people you've led will carry on without you."

During team meetings, he inspired us to seek aggressive goals for our careers. He was Caucasian and every manager was African-American, but that didn't matter to him. He didn't see race; he only saw human potential. "Each one of you qualifies to be a general manager. But getting the job will depend on who's hungry enough—who's willing to put in the effort and commitment. I want to see you all as general managers."

The next level after manager was the co-manager position. A co-manager reported to a general manager but ran the restaurant during times when the general manager didn't work. Desiree was our co-manager. She did a great job, and everyone knew she was slated to take Mark's job when he moved on.

After a year of working for Mark, my time came to be promoted. "You need to spread your wings, Ken," Mark said, smiling. "There's a co-manager position a few blocks away at the Franklin Street store, and we'd like you to take it."

I was stoked. I had succeeded at Wendy's, and my time at Aramark faded into a distant memory.

As my income increased, I decided to move out of Granny's apartment and rent my own place. I found an apartment near Granny's in the Courtway Building at 69th Street and Oglesby. But most important, the place was mine. I had a career and a home.

Now there was only one thing missing—Deidre.

Deidre and I continued to date while I worked at Wendy's. We were totally committed to each other and spent a great deal of time together. For Thanksgiving that year, I joined Deidre at her parents' house for dinner; I often hung out with Deidre's family during holiday celebrations. They were a stable family and had lived in the same home for over twenty years. Her parents had accepted me as one of the family, and I'm sure they assumed we would marry one day.

Deidre's Uncle Clint was also very cordial. After dinner that Thanksgiving, he and I watched television in the family room. "You're always hanging around. It's nice to have you here. But what're you going to do about the future?"

I gave him some vague answer, but his question

triggered something inside me.

As I rode the bus home that night, I kept thinking about his words. And I thought about Dee. *What am I going to do? Dee's an incredible woman—smart, supportive. And she balances me out. What am I waiting for?* It was time to settle down and permanently commit myself to the woman I loved.

On Valentine's Day 1990, I took Deidre to dinner at Red Lobster—her favorite restaurant. While she went to the ladies' room, I took a ring out of my pocket and placed it on her plate. When she returned, she saw the ring and screamed for joy. Then she immediately started bawling.

She placed the ring on her finger. It was a perfect fit.

On May 25, 1991, Deidre and I married. We'd come a long way from our senior trip to Orlando seven years earlier. At our wedding, Mark Burrell joined me as my best man. I felt blessed by God as I stood at the altar—between Mr. and Miss Personality of Willibrord Catholic High School.

chapter nineteen

MY NEXT PAID INTERNSHIP

*"If you work for a man, for heavens
sake work for him." — Kin Hubbard*

My general manager at the Franklin Street
Wendy's was not a strong leader. Tivia let
me run the place, which was fine, but I
still wanted to work for a leader who would guide me to the
next level.

Tivia had a ghetto mentality. She did drugs, and she
surrounded herself with friends from crack parties. They hung
out at the store, and Tivia ignored her responsibilities while
they were there. She was a *camper*. She probably earned more
money than she ever hoped to, and she lacked the motivation
to keep climbing.

While working there, I used everything Mark Ghee
had taught me. I adhered to the systems of quality. I reduced
service times. And I tried to inspire my managers and crew
chiefs to improve their performance and set aggressive career
goals.

But after a year, I grew restless. My passion for the job

dwindled. *I can't stay here much longer. I think my shelf life at Wendy's is up.*

One morning, I scurried around the store performing my usual tasks: encouraging the crew, wiping down tables in the dining area, and checking on my customers. As I worked, I thought about updating my résumé. *This time, I'll have something to show after graduation.* Thinking about the résumé reminded me of Dr. Ashraf at SIU. She'd encouraged her students to pursue internships as a way of gaining experience. *Wendy's has been a great internship. I've learned a lot. Now, it's time to try something new.*

After my experience at Aramark, I wanted to take ownership of my career. I didn't want to fall into a complacent attitude. *I won't become a camper. I'll treat every job as a paid internship. I'll learn everything I can, provide excellent service, and move on when the time is right.*

As I often did during breakfast, I grabbed a pot of coffee and took it out to the dining area to refill customers' cups. I usually smiled when walking through the dining area, and sometimes, I even sat down with guests for a minute if they welcomed conversation. That particular time, I refilled the cup of a middle-aged gentleman wearing a gray trench coat.

"Thank you," the man said. "You run a good place here."

Customers appreciated my attentiveness, and as a result, I did receive an occasional compliment. So, I thanked the man and returned to my work, not thinking any more about it.

About ten minutes later, the same man approached me as I wiped down tables. "My name's Dan Lechter." He handed me his business card. "I'm an operations director with Grandma Gephardt's Cookie Company."

Who?

"I like the way you manage this restaurant," he said. "And the way you interact with people. If you ever feel like making a change, give me a call."

"Thank you, sir. I appreciate your telling me that."

I slid the card in my pocket, and he said good-bye. But something stirred inside me. Moments earlier I'd thought about seeking new challenges.

That evening, I rode the bus home and stared at Mr. Lechter's business card. *This is more than a coincidence. I've gotta talk to this guy.*

The next morning, I called him.

"Have you ever heard of Grandma Gephardt's?" he asked.

"No, I'm afraid not."

"Well, we have twelve locations in major downtown buildings. We sell more than cookies. We also have restaurants that serve breakfast and lunch."

"No kidding?"

"We're growing, and I'm looking for general managers. From what I saw, I think you have the potential to be one."

That was all he had to say. *A general manager!* We scheduled an interview for the following week, and I updated my résumé to reflect my co-manager experience.

Mr. Lechter met me at their restaurant inside the Bank of Tokyo Building, where Grandma Gephardt's ran a 100-seat food court. The company, he explained, had been started by an entrepreneur in Minnesota. The founder, Larry Cerf, had graduated college with an engineering degree, but after graduation, he and a friend started the Wocka Tocka Moccasins Company in Wisconsin. The business took off, and he made a lot of money. But Mr. Cerf was an entrepreneur at heart, so he soon started another business. He took his grandmother's cookie recipe and sold cookies in shopping mall food courts. From there he expanded into muffins, bagels, and donuts. Before long, he offered full meals in business buildings throughout Minneapolis, St. Louis, and Chicago. He also sold frozen yogurt under a different name, Aunt Annie's Frozen Yogurt.

"We'd train you for a few months," Mr. Lechter said, "then we'd assign you as general manager of your own store. Our restaurants are only open Monday through Friday, so there'll be no weekend hours. We can start you at a salary of $21,000."

Another raise? Better hours? It's perfect.

As a child, Dad pushed me to pursue excellence and self-improvement. Mu'dear complemented that effort by believing the future held bright promises. Together, along with other instrumental people, they helped mold me into someone who had a passion for his work and a penchant for new possibilities.

I had received countless gifts, like attending college, working for Jack Beard, interning with Marriott, and learning from Mark Ghee. Later, I would even count my experience with Aramark as a blessing. *God has his own plans, and I have to be obedient to those plans. And to the people he sends my way.*

I reached across the table and shook Mr. Lechter's hand. "You've got yourself a new manager."

I started two weeks later, working at the restaurant inside the Mercantile Exchange building. The Mercantile Exchange was similar to the New York Stock Exchange, except at the Merc, futures were traded instead of stocks. It was the second largest futures exchange in the world, so it was always busy.

I reported to Tim Gergel, the general manager of the restaurant. It was one of their larger stores. At three o'clock each morning, a baker came in and prepared the muffins, donuts, bagels, and cookies. During the day, we served lunch from three stations—pizza, sandwiches, and Chinese food. We made everything out front where the customers could watch their food being prepared.

Tim trained me for two months. He was a friendly guy and well respected by Mr. Cerf. He was a lot like Jack Beard, because he also took the time to teach me every facet of the business. Being an entrepreneurial-type business, Grandma Gephardt's hadn't documented many of their processes like Wendy's had. So my training involved listening and watching Tim, and replicating what he did.

When Tim thought I'd learned enough of a particular aspect of the business, he stepped back and let me run things for a while. After I finished the training, he let me take over. "I'm going on vacation in a few weeks," he told me after my second month on the job. "You'll run the place while I'm gone."

I gathered all my notes together in a book and asked Tim a few remaining questions. When he left for his trip, I felt prepared. I managed the twenty employees for two weeks and kept the ship running like clockwork.

When Tim returned, he sat down and reviewed the performance numbers from the previous two weeks. He looked at me and smiled. "You did a great job, Ken. I'm proud of you."

The following week, Dan Lechter stopped in the store. "Ken, I've got a general manager opportunity at another location. Are you ready for it?"

"I was born ready."

Two days later, I started at a restaurant located in the Cigna Insurance building at 55 West Monroe Street. Mr. Lechter handed me a box of business cards. They read: "Ken Brown, General Manager." *One more management level to plug into my résumé.* The Aramark hole in my career history was looking smaller and smaller.

The restaurant wasn't as big as the Mercantile Exchange location; it only produced a fraction of the sales. But it was mine.

Within limits, I ran it the way I wanted to: I set the daily menu specials, implemented systems for food preparation and inventory control, and analyzed the profitability of different products and determined where to focus our attention.

Twice a week, I ordered my food supplies from Kurt, an account manager with Sysco Food Services. When he came in, I let him sit at my office desk. He'd pull out his laptop and say, "Okay, Ken, whaddya need?"

I'd go through the list.

When I finished, he'd give me some new ideas. He helped me be creative. "The sandwich shop down the street started selling bottle juice," he said. "They've been ordering a lot—seems to be doing real well." Or he might tell me about new products. "Tyson Foods has a new deli product. Do you want me to send the rep by to give you some samples?"

I knew he was trying to boost his sales, but he wanted to boost mine as well.

"If I sell you stuff that doesn't help your business, then you're going to go with someone else. I know that. I want us both to win."

He was like a breath of fresh air from the outside world, bringing all sorts of food ideas from suppliers and creative product ideas from different restaurants. He helped me think outside the box and consider new ways of generating revenue. His job intrigued me. I liked how it allowed him to bring value to other businesses.

One morning, I noticed a man delivering catering trays of bagels and muffins to an office in the building. *We should be doing that.*

I purchased a supply of trays and started delivering a free platter of muffins or cookies to many of the offices. "This is what we can do for you," I told them. "The next time you need something like this, please consider using us."

As far as I knew, Grandma Gebhardt's had never offered catering before, but I studied the costs and determined we could make money. It wasn't long before a few of the businesses ordered trays. We also provided coffee, which was very profitable.

When the office workers spotted us preparing or delivering the food, the number of orders grew. I hired additional workers, and catering became a major part of our business.

Each month, Dan came into the store and reviewed our sales figures from the previous month. The catering business took off so quickly I hadn't informed him what I was doing.

"Ken, what's up with these transactions? You're up twenty percent over last year. What's going on here?"

He was thrilled when I explained it to him. Then I mentioned some of the other ideas I wanted to explore. "I want to sell bottled juices. Some great products have come on the market, and I think my clientele will go for them."

He glanced at me from the corner of his eyes and smiled. "Okay. Go for it."

"I also want to offer pre-made salads. A lot of people exercise in the gym downstairs each morning, and sometimes they're going to want salads."

He put away the reports in a file folder. "Do what you want. It's your show, now."

I worked at Grandma Gebhardt's for a year and a half. Sales continued to grow during that time, and I was comfortable. But as usual, once I felt like I'd learned a job, I grew bored. I needed new challenges to maintain my passion.

chapter twenty

Jumping the Gun

In all thy ways acknowledge him, and he
shall direct thy path." — Proverbs 3:6

My restlessness with my Grandma Gebhardt's job led me to make an impulsive mistake. To learn more about the food business, I had started asking Kurt, my Sysco account manager, about his job. He explained that in addition to calling on restaurants, he also sold to hospitals and hotels. He walked me through the details of the food supply network. "The original manufacturers, like Tyson Foods, are called suppliers—or principals. Food brokers sell the suppliers' products to distributors like us. Then we sell and deliver those products to the end-users like you."

"So the other delivery trucks I see on the street—Kraft, Sexton—those are distributors, also?"

"Yes, but Sysco is the largest."

I was like a sponge—absorbing his information. The more I learned, the more I wanted to know. I also asked him about Sysco as a company.

"It's a great company. We have good hours, full benefits, and we make decent money. Most account managers start out around $30,000, but you can make more through commissions."

Grandma Gebhardt's had provided me a great paid internship. But I'd mastered my job, and because the company was so small, they couldn't offer much upward mobility.

I asked Kurt for a human resources contact within his company, and I updated my résumé—this time adding General Manager. In addition to contacting Sysco, I also sent my résumé to the other distributors—Kraft and Sexton.

When I told Deidre what I was doing, she smiled and rolled her eyes. "Here we go, again." She had come to expect my constant search for new challenges.

I held her hands and looked into her eyes. "Listen, Dee. I know the restaurant business. I can do a great job with a distributor. I can give them ideas. This feels right."

I was stunned when all three companies offered me an interview. At Sysco, I first talked with a district manager. I explained to him my passion for the food business and my familiarity with restaurants. And I demonstrated my knowledge of Sysco's business and the food network through the information Kurt had given me.

"Your résumé and knowledge are impressive," he said. "There are a few more people I'd like you to see."

After him, I interviewed with a regional manager, and finally, with a vice president. Both interviews went smooth.

When I finished with the vice president, he smiled and shook my hand. "Well, Ken, you're just the type of person we need in this company. You can add value to what we're doing. Our human resources department will call you in a few days to discuss the details of an offer."

I raced home to tell Deidre the great news. "I've got the job! This feels so right. I'm supposed to be there. It's the next level that the Lord has for me."

"I'm proud of you," she said.

It was a month before Christmas. *Thank you, God, for this early Christmas gift.* I could see his plan for my life coming together.

The next day, I phoned Kraft and Sexton to let them know. Then, I did one of the dumbest things I'd ever done. I called Dan Lechter and quit my job at Grandma Gebhardt's.

"I hate to see you go, but I understand," he said. "You've done a lot for us, and I appreciate it."

A week later, no one from Sysco had called to make an offer. I called and left a voicemail every other day. But I received no response. Another week passed. I finished my last day at Grandma Gebhardt's and still hadn't heard from Sysco. I tried not to worry. *They said I was exactly the type of person they needed. They said they'd call. I have to believe that.*

Finally, a week before Christmas, a Sysco human resources manager returned my call. "We haven't forgotten about you. We've experienced a few changes here. Some of the people you interviewed with have been transferred, and you got lost in the shuffle. But hold tight. You'll hear from us soon."

I glanced at the calendar and realized they wouldn't do anything until after the holidays. *It'll be another two weeks before I hear anything.*

I tried to remain confident through Christmas and New Year's, but I was getting a bad feeling. During the first week of January, I called the HR manager and got him.

"There've been a lot of changes here," he said. "I'm

afraid we've decided not to bring you on board."

"No way." *I've gotta come on board. I've already quit my job. I've told everyone.*

"I'm sorry."

After I said good-bye, I slammed down the phone. "I can't believe it!" I paced around the kitchen. "They lied! They said they would hire me!"

I spent most of that day in shock and anger. But as the hour approached for Deidre to come home, I realized how irresponsible I had been. *This is my fault. I had no right to quit without an offer. I'm a husband now, and I can't be so rash.*

Deidre worked as a teacher with the Chicago Public Schools, so we still had some income, but it didn't cover all our expenses. In addition, we'd started the process of buying a townhouse in the suburb of Aurora. *How stupid could I be?*

When Deidre arrived home, I told her that the Sysco job didn't work out. I stared at the floor as I spoke.

"You've been through this before," she said, touching my cheek, "and everything worked out. Have faith. You're a determined man, and you'll find something."

Her faith motivated me to immediately search for another job. This time, I wasn't going to mope around. *Your paid internship days are over. You need money.*

A few days later, I spotted an advertisement in the Want Ads for a Wendy's manager. *I've done that. I could do it again.* I called the number and, after an interview, got the job.

This Wendy's was located in Schaumburg and an owner/operator, Steve Wilt, ran it. The Wendy's corporation owned the previous locations where I worked, but this store was a franchise. Steve had once served as a regional vice president with Wendy's, but he had decided to go into business for himself. The corporation assisted with the financing, and Steve bought three stores.

While I worked there, I observed Steve as he came into the store each day. He drove up in his silver Jaguar around lunchtime and touched base with us. He was tall with gray, slicked-back hair. He knew all of his employees and many of his customers. We followed Wendy's strict food preparation processes, but as a franchise, Steve had a lot of freedom on how he ran his business.

I'd like to be a business owner someday. But it'll never happen as long as I stay here.

My heart wasn't in the job. Steve already employed a general manager at each store, so there was no upward mobility. And my job didn't present any new challenges. *I've taken a step backwards.*

I didn't talk about my work situation with most people. I knew that my mother-in-law had already expressed concerns about my stability. *I can only imagine what the rest of my family and friends think.*

After three months at Wendy's, I humbled myself and called Kraft Foods. My voice quivered as I spoke. "Sysco decided not to bring anyone on board. Are you still interested in talking?"

"Sure," they said. "Come on in."

I went in to their district office and interviewed with the district manager, Bob Marchioni. "Why should I hire you?" he asked.

"Because I'm hungry," I said. He had no idea how hungry I really was. "And I know the restaurant business. I'll be able to add value for our customers while making sales for us."

At the end of the interview, he said, "I think you'd be

a good fit for us. We'll be in contact."

I've heard that before.

But a few days later, I did get a call from Mr. Marchioni. "We'd like to hire you as an account executive. We'll start you off with a base salary of $30,000."

Yes! Thank you, Lord.

I felt bad quitting my job at Wendy's, but I didn't have the passion I needed to excel.

On my first day at Kraft, Bob gave me business cards—Ken Brown, Account Executive—and assigned me a sales territory that included the Joliet and Riverbolt areas. I would sell to restaurants and hospitals, and a few day care centers.

Bob mentored me and oversaw my training. For added motivation, he played videos for me by Les Brown—an internationally-known inspirational speaker. Les Brown is an African-American who grew up in impoverished circumstances, but today he's a successful author and entrepreneur. His passion and drive for excellence reminded me of my father.

Through the training, Bob introduced me to a whole new aspect of the food business. And he introduced me to a man who would, one day, become one of the most important people in my life.

"This is Chuck Goldberg from AWG," Bob said, motioning to the man standing next to him. "He's a food broker and represents a lot of the products we distribute."

We shook hands.

"I'd like you to come out to his office tomorrow," Mr. Goldberg told me, "so I can show you our products. You up for that?"

"That'd be great."

The next day, he picked me up and drove me up to Vernon Hills, a ritzy area north of Chicago. Their office was located near the Chicago Bears training facility and a lot of the football players lived in the area. I gawked at the fancy homes as we passed them.

After arriving at the AWG office, Mr. Goldberg ushered me into their boardroom. He offered me a seat and left for a moment. I sat down in one of the high-back leather chairs and set my notepad on the long cherry table. I looked around the room; plush burgundy carpet covered the floor and award plaques adorned the walls.

I walked over and scanned the inscriptions on the awards. *Impressive.* They were from a wide variety of companies, such as Tyson, Sara Lee, Quaker, Nabisco, and Simplot. Simplot, I later learned, provided McDonald's with French fries.

Mr. Goldberg returned with a basket of chicken and a drink. "This a new chicken product by Tyson. It's called Honey Stung Chicken and tastes incredible. And the drink is a new juice product from Tropicana called Tropicana Twisters." He also brought some other food like some Simplot fries and Rich's Cookies and set them in front of me. "Help yourself."

I was hungry, and the food tasted great.

We talked for half an hour and hit it off. I told him about my background, and he told me about the company. When we finished, he played a video about the company and brought out more food. He knew how to treat his distributors well.

Several years passed before I ran into Chuck again, but I still made every effort to introduce AWG products to my customers. I didn't use heavy-handed tactics, though. Instead,

I served my clients by taking time with them, asking questions, and learning as much as I could about their business. I studied their menus and discovered their needs. I knew what it was like to run a restaurant, and I wanted my customers be successful. Over time, I built an impressive record of sales.

"I'm doing this charity event," my fraternity brother, Gary Heflin, told me. "It's called *Real Men Cook*. You're in the food industry; you should do it with me." Kofi and Yvette Moyo had started *Real Men Cook* a few years earlier to highlight positive African-American male role models. Black men were usually portrayed negatively in the media, so the Moyos, who ran a promotions and marketing company, wanted to hold an event to counter the negative images.

On Father's Day each year, a hundred or so African-American men gathered at a downtown facility and cooked meals. The general public paid $20 to enter the event and partake of the different foods. The Moyos donated the proceeds to a different cause each year, like the YMCA.

The first year I participated in *Real Men Cook*, I was hooked. The camaraderie and playful competition between the men was fun, and it felt good to participate in a worthy cause.

The second year, Lawry's Seasonings became a major sponsor of the event. To add a little competition, Lawry's held a contest for the top three dishes that were prepared using their seasonings.

I tweaked a broccoli chicken recipe I'd used at Grandma Gebhardt's. I added some Lawry's seasoning and called it: Ken Brown's World Famous Broccoli Chicken.

Some of the men cooked a good portion of their food

beforehand, but I made my entire dish on site. I brought the chicken along in a cooler and used a wok to cook everything. I cut up the broccoli, added green and red bell peppers, and let the chicken marinate in a garlic sauce.

People came by, and I let them eat it right out of the wok. Deidre and Mu'dear also came with me.

"Your chicken explodes with flavor," Mu'dear said after tasting some.

When it was over, I cleaned up my wok and dishes while a woman from Lawry's announced the winners. I didn't pay much attention, until I heard the woman say, "Ken Brown."

I looked up, and the man next to me shouted, "You won!"

I couldn't believe it. The whole place cheered. Deidre hugged me. A reporter from the *Chicago Tribune* came over to interview me, and a photographer took my picture.

While I talked to the reporter, I spied Deidre chuckling lightheartedly and shaking her head. "Here we go again," she seemed to be saying.

The next morning, I opened the newspaper and found the article about the *Real Men Cook* event. It included my name and mentioned I was an account executive with Kraft. Next to the article was a photograph of me wearing a first place medal and holding an oversized check for $500.

It felt great to be recognized for something outside of work. But after a few weeks, I didn't think much more about it. That is, until I received a phone call.

"Hey, Ken. This is Larry Cerf from Grandma Gebhardt's. I saw your picture in the paper."

"Really?"

"So you're with Kraft, now. How's it going?"

"Excellent. It's going excellent. I'm enjoying this side of the business."

"I'm glad to hear it. Hey, if you're up for it, I'd like to meet with you. I have an opportunity you might be interested in."

chapter twenty-one

BIGGER
AND BETTER

The greatest thing in the world is not so much
where we are, but in what direction we are moving."
— Oliver Wendell Holmes

"The job is yours if you want it, Ken. I'll pay you $35,000, and I'll give you a company car. Plus, I'll give you an American Express to cover fuel and meal expenses."

Larry had flown me to Minnesota to meet with him and his sales manager, Brian Keenan. *No one's ever recruited me like this before. This is sweet!*

Larry was Caucasian, and in his mid-forties. He was of medium height and very fit. He wore a casual blazer with an open neck Oxford shirt. "I want to expand my Annie's Frozen Yogurt products into the Chicago market," he said. "I think you're just the person to do it."

In addition to his Grandma Gebhardt's stores, Mr. Cerf sold his lines of cookies and frozen yogurt through distributors to end-users such as restaurants, colleges, hotels, and hospitals. He had penetrated the Minnesota market through the sales efforts of Brian, and now Larry wanted to grow into other markets. His main competitor in frozen yogurt was Columbo, which was owned by Nestlé Foods. Annie's Frozen Yogurt was creamier and richer, but with Nestlé's size and financial strength, Columbo dominated the market.

"I wouldn't do this if I didn't believe in the product," Larry said. "I can't make any promises about success, but this would give you an opportunity to start on the ground floor of something exciting."

Larry wined and dined me. We went to a fancy restaurant for dinner and then another for lunch the next day. He took me on a plant tour of the Kohler Dairy where the frozen yogurt was manufactured, and he walked me around his offices to meet the staff.

The compensation package he offered astounded me. With the extras, I would more than double my income since being fired from Aramark.

But, I was happy at Kraft. I'd worked there just long enough to establish a good reputation, and I wanted to make a name for myself within that company.

When the visit wrapped up, I thanked Larry for the offer. "Can I have the weekend to think about it?"

"No problem. I'll call you on Monday."

I fidgeted on the flight home. *What should I do?*

I'd gained a reputation among some of my family and friends as someone who couldn't hold a job. Deidre's mother, in particular, questioned my stability. "Do you think *this* one will work?" she asked when I joined Kraft.

If I leave now, she's really going to doubt that I'm a good husband for her daughter. *I thought about the last time I tried to make a job change and left a comfortable situation.* That didn't work out so well. Maybe it would be safer to stay put.

But as I watched the clouds pass by and scanned the

horizon, I didn't feel like playing it safe. *I'm just Kenny from the block. But look how far I've come.*

I trusted Larry. He was an entrepreneur, and the more I'd worked around restaurants, the more I wanted to run my own business some day. *This opportunity would give me a chance to create something new, even if it isn't mine.*

Plus, Larry respected me. He didn't ask for a résumé; he already knew what I could do. He thought I could add value. By the time the plane landed, I couldn't wait to tell Deidre about the offer.

At first, she seemed hesitant. "But things have always worked out before," she said later. "Maybe you should take it."

On Saturday, I attended my high school's tenth reunion. As I ate dinner with Deidre, Mark Burrell, and other friends, I thought about how far I'd come in ten years. *I've gained something from every job. I would've missed out on a lot if I'd stayed at Aramark and gotten comfortable.*

I closed my eyes and pictured working for Larry. *This is what I'm supposed to do. This is part of God's plan.* As I often did, I heard Mu'dear's voice. "Bigger and better. The next one will be bigger and better."

Larry called on Monday, and I accepted the job.

Larry flew me back to Minnesota and said I could drive my new car home after the visit. I spent the next two days with Brian. He was a tall man with a ruddy complexion and sandy hair. A true salesman, he'd worked at Proctor and Gamble for many years before joining Grandma Gebhardt's. He was intense and methodical as he trained me on the sales process.

Brian reviewed the product details, including the financial information. Then he took me on sales calls in his territory. While he drove, he explained that in Chicago, Nestlé seemed to have a lock on the frozen yogurt market. Nestlé paid a lot of money to distributors like Kraft and Sysco so they'd carry the Nestlé line of products. "We lack the funds to compete head-to-head with Nestlé. We can't buy our way into the distributors; instead, we'll have to go through the back door. We want you to sell directly to the restaurants and other users and have them order from the distributors. Hopefully, we can create enough demand to attract the distributors' attention."

We drove to different locations in his new Pontiac Grand Am. It had a maroon interior and a new car smell. *This is nice. I wonder what my car will be like.* I expected something much smaller, but I didn't care. I was just grateful to stop riding the bus.

After we finished and returned to the office, Brian asked me to complete some administrative paperwork. "While you're doing that, I'll get your car ready."

About half an hour later, he returned and tossed me the keys. We walked outside, and he pointed to the white Grand Am we'd been driving the previous two days. "There she is." It hadn't been his car after all.

The car sparkled from its recent washing. "Awesome!"

"And here's your card." He handed me a new American Express card.

At the bottom it read: "Kenneth Brown, Grandma Gebhardt's Cookie Company."

I drove home on I-94 and cranked up the radio. The

summer heat radiated off the asphalt, and I rolled down the window, feeling the hot air blow across my face. I couldn't stop smiling. *I'm just little Kenny from the block. But look at me now!*

For the next year, I worked hard to establish a market share in Chicago for Annie's Frozen Yogurt and Grandma Gebhardt's Cookies. I set up an office in my home, stocked a freezer in my garage full of frozen yogurt and cookie samples, and used my laptop to plan cold calls on potential clients.

As always, I brought a lot of energy to my job. And I developed unique ways to sell my products. Annie's had a better flavor profile and better packaging, and it cost less. But restaurants sometimes showed reluctance to trying something new. When a restaurant resisted trying Annie's, I offered to perform a taste test for their customers.

"I'll come in on your busiest day and set up a taste test. If your customers prefer Annie's over Columbo, will you buy Annie's?"

"Absolutely," they usually said.

I enjoyed running the taste tests. I'd set up a fancy table next to a large neon sign with the Annie's logo. And I'd give away trinkets like key chains, pens, and little footballs. Time after time, the majority of taste testers preferred Annie's.

After the demonstration, the customer usually agreed to order Annie's. But a week or two later, I'd stop to see the same customer and often notice them serving Columbo's again. "I thought you were going to order Annie's."

"We did. But Sysco still ships us Columbo."

When I talked to the distributors, they told me their company wouldn't stock Annie's, so they had to deliver what they had in their warehouse. I was stuck in a catch-22. We didn't have the money to buy our way into distributors, and the distributors wouldn't listen to the preferences of their customers. We did make a few inroads. We sold the cookies to a few school systems, which became instant high volume customers. But overall, I wasn't closing the number of sales I wanted to.

However, good news at home soon compensated for the lack of good news at work. On a cool morning in April, Dee wrapped her arms around me and said, "You're gonna be a daddy!"

I was stoked. A father would be the most important job I'd ever have. And at least one job I'd keep forever.

A year after I started with Grandma Gebhardt's, Larry flew down to Chicago and met me at the downtown Westin hotel. We reviewed our sales and market share reports.

"I'm sorry to say this, Ken, but we're not making enough penetration into this market. I can't afford to keep going."

"I'm trying everything I can think of," I said.

"You're doing great. It's not your fault. Our competitors have us locked out."

Here we go again. My stomach tightened, and my forehead started to sweat. I thought about Dee and the baby. "Mr. Cerf, my wife is four months preg—"

"Don't worry about a thing. I'm going to give you six months severance pay. And you can keep the car and credit card during that time."

I relaxed. Everything would be okay. "Thank you, sir.

I'm flattered you brought me into your company, and I hope I added some value."

"Hey, it's the least I can do. You're an excellent salesman. This project just wasn't meant to be."

I drove home from the meeting and thought about what had just happened. *I think I just got fired again, but I don't feel that bad.* Through my evictions and other periods of unemployment, I'd grown accustomed to a certain level of instability. God had never abandoned me. He always made things work out in the end.

I had learned a lot about sales from Brian and about the business from a manufacturer's viewpoint. Now I had six months to find another job. I didn't know how that would happen, but I believed I'd find something worthwhile. Being unemployed with a baby on the way should have stressed me out. But those six months were some of the most peaceful times of my life. They were a gift.

Best of all, I got to help Dee during her pregnancy. I accompanied her to doctor's appointments and got to see my son through the ultrasound. *He's a miracle.* I knew full well how much impact a parent can have on one's life. *I hope I'll be a good parent.*

Although she worried about our finances, Deidre was patient as I searched for a new job. I think she enjoyed having the extra help as her due date approached. I didn't tell anyone else about being laid off. I still had the company car, and I still had some loose ends to tie up. Some of my customers needed help with their orders, and I had already committed to attend a few more tradeshows.

One day, as I worked the booth at my final tradeshow, a man walked up to my table.

"Well, well. Ken Brown. How're you doing?"

I looked up from dishing out frozen yogurt samples. It was Chuck Goldberg—the man from AWG who, when I started with Kraft, took me to his office in Vernon Hills and treated me so nice.

"So you're working for a manufacturer now?" he said.

We talked for a few minutes, and I told him what I'd been doing. As he started to leave, I asked, "You looking for any good people, Mr. Goldberg?"

"Always. Always, Mr. Brown." He handed me his business card and told me to give him a call.

chapter twenty-two

THINKING OUTSIDE THE BOX

"He who does not climb the mountain cannot see the view." — Chinese Proverb

On a windy day in March of 1996, I drove to AWG's offices in Vernon Hills and met Mr. Goldberg for an interview. I entered the office and passed the conference room where, two years earlier, he fed me those great samples.

"Thanks again for taking such good care of me that day," I said.

Chuck was a short man with red hair and freckles. He took a drink from his bottle of Dannon water, which he always kept with him. "No problem. I know how hard you worked on our behalf."

"Yeah, check your numbers. I sold a lot of Honey Stung Chicken and Tropicana."

He smiled. "Thanks. I appreciate that."

The interview went well, and a week later he called. "I'd like to hire you as a sales and marketing consultant. I'll start you out at a base salary of $40,000."

While he spoke, I wrote down the salary figure on a notepad and held it out to Deidre.

She shook her head. "Wow."

"I have a plan for you," Chuck said. "We're not penetrating the south side, and I want to see what you can do."

I knew south Chicago had a bad reputation in the food sales business. "Don't bother going south of Soldier Field," some salesmen said. "People don't buy over there."

A lot of industry sales people were white. In fact, all my new colleagues at AWG were white and older than I, and they might've been afraid to try to develop that area. But I was young and hungry, and I knew the territory.

AWG was the product of a recent merger between two family companies: Asmussen and Associates and The Waxler Group. Combined, they became one of the largest food brokers and represented prominent principals (meaning food manufacturers) such as Tyson, Sara Lee, Quaker, Nabisco, Tropicana, and Dannon. They represented so many companies that we could go into almost any food business and have something to offer.

During World War II, Roy Asmussen Sr., met and befriended Ray Kroc, the future leader of McDonald's. After the war, they went their separate ways until Mr. Asmussen started brokering for a company called Simplot, who had just developed a process for quick freezing vegetables. Mr. Asmussen sold Mr. Kroc on Simplot's frozen, sliced potatoes, and with a handshake agreement, started a relationship to provide McDonald's its French fries. That business relationship still continues today, and makes up a significant portion of AWG's business. Roy Asmussen Sr.'s grandson, Mick, now ran the company, and Chuck, who came from the Waxler Group, managed the sales effort.

I admired Chuck, and he became a true friend. Chuck was Jewish, and I learned a lot about the Jewish culture by working for him. When I was a kid, Dad exposed me to Jewish people and introduced me to their eating choices and lifestyle, but now I learned about them on a whole new level. For observant Jews, I learned how important it was for them to pay attention to how they spoke, the way they dressed, what foods they put into their body, how much exercise they got, and how they managed their finances. As a Jewish man, Chuck was most concerned with achieving excellence. He didn't care what anyone's skin color was, he just expected you to excel at your job and treat people fairly.

Chuck trained me on AWG's portfolio of products and their sales techniques. "It's important to think outside the box," he said. "Sales often come from approaching your tasks creatively."

Chuck taught me important people skills. He remembered people's names, and he asked about their families. He was sincere; he really cared about them.

As I started to make sales, he left notes of encouragement on my desk: "Great sale, Ken! Keep up the good work."

During part of my training, I traveled to different manufacturing plants, including a turkey processing plant in Michigan, a chicken plant in Arkansas, and a Simplot potato processing center in Idaho. The manufacturing system

Simplot employed to make the French fries amazed me.

As a guide led me on a tour, I watched trucks arrive and dump dirty potatoes into a large bin. They came out of the bin completely peeled. Then they slid down a chute with water where machines sliced, dried, and quick-froze them. At the end of the process, conveyors dumped the fries into boxes, and dockworkers prepared them for shipment. On one side of the viewing platform, the fries were dumped into a variety of boxes for shipment to different customers; but on the other side, the fries fell into thousands of boxes labeled with the McDonald's golden arches. At the time, I had no idea how involved I'd be with those fries in the future.

After my initial training, I focused on developing clients on the south side of Chicago. Usually, the distributors took the sales lead—when a distributor tried to sell a customer on a particular AWG product, they might ask us to visit the customer to review the product's features and benefits. But I didn't want to wait for other salespeople, so I cold-called customers on my own.

I worked hard and made sales. Instead of distributor reps calling me, I called and told them to place an order. When I sold Louie's Market one million pound of Simplot fries, I knew I'd hit my stride.

"Congratulations on the Louie's deal," Chuck said in a note. "I'm proud of you."

After nine months on the job, Chuck approached me with a special request. "Ken, you've done an excellent job these last few months. I'm glad I brought you on. Now, I'm looking to add another salesperson, and I need someone just like you. Do you know anyone?"

"I sure do—my friend Archie."

Archie Tolar was a friend of mine from SIU; he'd

majored in Food and Nutrition along with me. My job changes had always interested him. "Where you working now? What are you learning?" Archie possessed an entrepreneurial spirit like mine, and he seemed to live vicariously through each of my new job adventures.

Chuck interviewed Archie and hired him. It felt great to pass along some of my good fortune to someone else.

I proved we could sell on the south side, and I earned a good reputation within AWG. But there was one restaurant I hadn't tried selling, yet. Every day as I drove home, I passed *Charlie Robinson's Ribs* in Oak Park. Nobody could ever get an appointment with Mr. Robinson; he was known as a recluse and wouldn't even let his own distributor rep visit him.

I talked to his Sysco sales rep about going to *Robinson's Ribs* for a joint visit.

"No way," Shawn said. "He doesn't want to see anyone."

But Mr. Robinson intrigued me. He owned four restaurants, and I knew he used a lot of chicken and cooked a lot of fries. *If I can sell to him, then I'll be The Man.* I was up for the challenge.

One evening on my way home, I stopped at the Woodridge restaurant. I grabbed a table and studied the menu, hoping Mr. Robinson would come out. When he didn't, I walked up to the counter in the lobby and asked to see him.

"He's not here right now," the woman said.

"Please tell him that Ken Brown with AWG stopped by to talk to him."

"What business do you have with him?"

"I just wanted to talk to him about his restaurants."

"Well, he's not here right now, but I'll pass along the message."

I sat down at the table and ordered some ribs. While I waited for my food, I glanced around the restaurant and took notes on things I saw. I watched how many orders of chicken they processed. He also sold muffins. *He might be interested in some of Tyson's or Sara Lee's products.* Another thing I noticed were the four security cameras positioned around the edge of the ceiling.

All of a sudden, a man walked toward me. I knew it was Mr. Robinson because his face matched the face on the barbeque bottle sitting on my table. He was a tall, thin African-American man. "You Ken Brown?"

"Yes, sir."

"You decided to wait? Whaddya want?"

"I'm with AWG, and I wanted to meet you. Your rep said you don't see salespeople, but I wanted a bite to eat and thought I might run into you."

He stared at me, and his eyebrows furrowed as he studied me. "Whaddya got?"

I pulled out my catalog of principals from my briefcase. "You use a lot of chicken breasts, don't you?"

"Yeah. So?"

My heart beat faster, but I kept talking. "How do you buy those?" As I talked, I kept looking up at those security cameras. It dawned on me that he'd probably spied on me through the cameras, and when he didn't see me leave, he came to see what I wanted.

"I buy them at market," he said, meaning he bought them at whatever prices the market bore on any given day.

"That's a big item for you, isn't it?"

"It's my number one item."

"Wouldn't you like to control those costs?"

"Absolutely."

"Then I got the product that can help you do that: Tyson's Flattened IQF Chicken Breast." *I can't believe I'm actually engaging Mr. Robinson in a sales conversation. Everyone said it was impossible.*

"How much more would that cost me?"

"Compared to this week's market price it would only be a few pennies more. But next week, if market prices go up, it would cost you less. I can give you a fixed price for Tyson's chicken for the next week, month, or year."

Mr. Robinson leaned back in his chair and put his hand to his chin.

"How many cases do you go through in a day?" I asked.

"Ten."

My jaw dropped.

"And that doesn't count my catering orders. I go through another five cases a day in catering jobs."

Wow. "How about trying our chicken on your next catering job. I'll add five cases to your truck delivery for tomorrow. You'll see it on your invoice, but it will have a zero price next to it. I'm going to pay for it. Would that be okay?"

"Sure. Go ahead."

Yes! "Okay, I'm going to call your rep and place the order. Do you have a phone I can use?"

"Follow me." Mr. Robinson took me back to his office and motioned toward his phone. He had a large office with a sofa and sitting area, along with his own private washroom and backdoor entrance. Against one wall were four security television monitors. *They said he wouldn't even talk to me, and now I'm in his office.*

I called Shawn, the Sysco rep. "I need you to put five cases of Tyson's Flattened IQF Chicken Breasts on the next delivery for Charlie Robinson."

"What? Are you sure?"

"Yep. I'm here in his office. He's sitting next to me."

"No way!"

I got off the phone, and Mr. Robinson looked over my catalog of principals. "What else you got there?"

"I've got a lot of products we can talk about, but I want to make sure we take care of your chicken first. That's your biggest item. We'll see how they work for you, then we can talk about some other possibilities."

The next day, Mr. Robinson called. "I like the chicken. Can you get me five more cases?"

"Sure thing. I'll even bring them over myself."

When I was growing up, my father drilled into me that life was ten percent what happened to me and ninety percent how I responded. Chuck had assigned me a territory with a reputation for not producing sales, but I didn't accept the conventional wisdom. I knew I could sell on the south side if I took chances and an aggressive approach.

A few days after my sale to Mr. Robinson, I called Dad and told him about my progress.

"That's my boy!" he said.

chapter twenty-three

SNATCHING THE PEARL

Excellence is doing a common thing in an uncommon way." — Booker T. Washington

I didn't follow up with Mr. Robinson right away. I didn't want to pressure him. A few days after he received those first two shipments, his Sysco rep called me. "Mr. Robinson just ordered twenty-five cases of Tyson's chicken," Shawn said. "I can't believe it."

The following week, I stopped in *Charlie Robinson's Ribs* and asked to speak with Mr. Robinson. This time when I gave the lady my name, she replied, "Just a moment. He'll be right with you."

He came out a minute later. "Hey, my people loved that chicken. They didn't have to de-bone it or pound it out." He pointed at my briefcase. "What else you got for me?"

"Well, I'd like to get to know your business before we talk about other products."

"Sure. Come on back to my office."

Over the next several weeks, I dropped in to see Mr. Robinson and give him some samples. He told me about his business. He shared information about his four restaurants, how much revenue each store produced and the various challenges he faced. He also told me about his catering activities and the vendor business he ran at Chicago Bears' games. As he spoke, I took notes and jotted down ideas on how I could help improve things.

I visited Mr. Robinson about once a week, and over time, we developed a great working relationship. I earned his trust, and he bought my products in large quantities. As I got to know his business, the entrepreneurial bug in me reared its head again. *I want to do this someday.* More and more, I visualized my dream. I pictured a little building with a sign in front of it: Ken's Hot Dogs. It wouldn't be much, but it'd be mine.

I didn't let my vision stand in the way of performing well at AWG, though. Who knew how long it'd be before I made my dreams a reality? I continued to work hard on the south side and make sales. Lots of them.

Chuck accompanied me on sales calls only once, but he followed my performance through the standard water cooler talk. "I hear good things about you, Ken."

Although I appreciated the feedback and the positive comments people made, it bugged me that I didn't have any quantifiable way of gauging my progress. My past employers had used numerical ways of measuring my performance. But with AWG, we never actually recorded sales. We just brokered—or assisted—the transactions. The distributor usually processed the sales.

There's no record of what I'm doing. How will I stand out when it comes time for them to evaluate my performance?

The other forty or so AWG sales representatives were older and better established than I. They had a track record.

I want to make sure I keep my job. I figured if I had contributed enough profit to cover my salary, then they'd keep me.

As I considered different ways of tracking my performance, I discovered a box of rarely used triplicate order forms in a storage closet. I grabbed a stack and took them with me on every sales call. If I called an order into a distributor, then I'd duplicate the item information and quantity on my form. I also recorded the distributor's transaction number, and that helped me track the order to make sure they filled it properly. I now had a way to gauge my progress.

The time for annual personnel reviews came at the end of the year. The tone in the office changed dramatically as the reviews approached. Normally, everyone maintained a friendly, family atmosphere, but as the evaluations began, my colleagues became tense. The appraisals, I learned, determined the amount of a person's raise for the following year.

I kept a relaxed attitude simply because I didn't have any expectations. *I received my raise when Chuck hired me.* I could've earned $40,000 for the next few years and been happy. I knew from office talk that the raises usually ranged from zero up to $1,000. *Anything additional I get is just a bonus.*

It was Chuck's job to evaluate all the sales and marketing people, and one by one, my counterparts filed into his office. When they exited, I could usually tell how things went. Some smiled when they returned to their desk, but others muttered angry comments under their breath.

I'd faced unemployment three times in my brief career, and I didn't want to take anything for granted. I didn't care about the raise; I just wanted to make sure Chuck's evaluation was accurate. *It's not really fair for him to review me. He's seen so little firsthand of what I do. Maybe I can give him some data on my sales.* So, in preparing for my meeting, I collected all my completed order forms and compiled the sales figures.

Whenever we had made a presentation to a large client, we assembled a professional binder full of information on our principals and the products they offered. I took that idea, and typed up a report of my sales. I compiled the information in a binder and sorted it by principal. I divided the sections with labeled tabs and introduced each principal with a cover sheet that contained the principal's logo and a photograph of their primary food item. On the cover of the binder, I added AWG's logo and titled the report: "Ken Brown, Rookie Year Review."

When it came time for my evaluation, Chuck called me into his office. I carried my briefcase with me, which contained two copies of my report.

Chuck sat behind a large oak desk. Hanging on his walls he had picture frames or plaques that contained various quotes about success. "Success is a journey, not a destination." "The journey of a thousand miles begins with the first step."

He asked how I liked working for AWG and about my family. He looked me in the eyes and smiled as I spoke. I knew he cared.

"Well, you've worked hard this year and really made some inroads. I can't tell you how much I appreciate your being on board."

"Thank you, Chuck. I'm glad you gave me the opportunity."

He pulled out a single sheet of paper and set it on the desk in front of me. It was a job evaluation form. Some of the items on the form were subjective, like "works well with others" and "commitment to the job."

"I think you did a great job this year," Chuck said. "I'm going to give you a $1,500 raise."

Sweet!

"You should know—that's the largest one I gave this year."

"Thank you, Chuck. I'm honored."

The money was icing on the cake. Not only was my job secure, but Chuck had recognized me as one of the best salespeople in the company.

At that point, a smarter man would've politely ended the meeting. But I'd put too much work into my report, and I wanted Chuck to have an accurate picture of the value I'd added.

"I'm glad you think I've done a good job," I said.

He leaned back in his chair and smiled.

"But there's something I want you to see." I pulled out the report and placed it on his desk.

He stopped smiling. He leaned forward and looked at the cover. Then he opened it to the Tyson section and glared at the Tyson logo and the picture of a chicken. He turned the next page hard.

Oh, no. He's getting angry. This isn't supposed to tick him off.

I cleared my throat. "I've kept track of my sales and organized them by principal. I wondered how you'd measure my performance, so I came up with this report. I thought it might be helpful in showing my progress."

He stared at me. He clenched his jaw and his eyes narrowed.

Great. I've blown it.

He glanced back at the report and flipped each page as hard as the first. I felt his anger rising. He stared at me again. "Why'd you do this?"

"Well, like I just said, because—"

"Be honest with me. Did you do this for money?"

"No. No, Chuck." My voice shook. "I just wanted you to know that I'm earning my keep."

He stood up. "We're going to have to table this for now. Can I keep this?" He picked up the report.

"Sure. That's for you. I have my own copy."

We shook hands. "Thanks for the raise. I really appreciate it."

As I walked out of the office, Chuck called after me. "Come back in Monday at eight, and we'll talk some more."

I drove home that day not knowing how to feel. I'd just received the largest dollar increase in the sales force, but I'd also shot myself in the foot. His request for me to come in Monday morning reminded me of the same one Mary made before she fired me.

I was restless all weekend and didn't sleep well. Monday morning, I returned to the office. Usually the salespeople only came in Fridays, so the place was quiet. Chuck called me into his office at eight o'clock.

"How was your weekend?" he asked.

"Fine, sir." I lied.

We engaged in small talk for a few minutes, and then Chuck came to the point. "Thirty people have marched into this office over the last few weeks and gone through this process. With each one, I just gave them something, and they accepted it."

He pulled my report out of his briefcase and set it on the desk. "Do you remember the television show, Kung Fu?"

I nodded. *Where's he going with this?*

"You'll remember that the main character, Caine, learned martial arts as a boy. Each episode started with a flashback as the young Caine learned a lesson from his master. In one episode, in order to improve Caine's reflexes, the master had Caine try to snatch a pearl from the master's hand."

Chuck smiled. It was good to see him smile again.

"I feel like you came in here on Friday and snatched the pearl from my hands."

"I don't follow you."

"That $1,500 I promised you on Friday," he said, "forget it. I've looked over your report. I'm making your raise $8,000."

My mouth gaped open, and I blinked hard. "What? Are you sure? That's unbelievable."

"I'm positive. You're worth it."

It was one of my proudest moments. And it made me regard Chuck even more highly. He could've stayed mad. He could've glanced at the report and thrown it away. Instead, he probably sat down with a calculator and added up the brokerage I'd brought in. And calculating the figure, he changed his mind.

When Chuck handed me the new evaluation form with the $8,000 figure, it felt like a crowning achievement. That evening, I told Deidre the great news. She hugged me and her eyes sparkled. "I'm proud of you. All of your determination has paid off."

Right before Christmas, AWG held its annual end-of-year banquet. I had seen a few *Salesperson of the Year* plaques hanging on the walls in the office, and I knew Chuck awarded it at the banquet.

"I'm going to win that award," I told Deidre. "After the raise I just received, I can't image not winning it." I obsessed over that award for several days.

"Don't think about it so much. It isn't that important," Deidre said.

"Yes, it is!"

"Well, don't get overconfident. You might not win it."

She had a point. I tried not to think about it, but as the youngest salesperson in the office, I wanted to prove myself to my peers.

The banquet was a beautiful affair. They held it in a hotel ballroom and treated us to a gourmet meal and wine. All the officers of the company spoke.

When it was time to announce the award, Chuck went to the podium. I immediately felt my stomach flutter with anticipation.

"We had many people in the running for *Salesperson of the Year*," Chuck said.

I became more excited and could barely contain myself. I wasn't arrogant—just thrilled at the opportunity to be recognized. At one point, I stopped listening to what he said and just waited for my name to be announced.

"So, without further ado, this year's award goes to…"

I took my napkin off my lap and placed it on the table. I was ready to stand.

"…Marissa Morrison."

What? I glanced at Dee and mouthed, "Huh?"

She rolled her eyes as if to say, "I told you so."

Later, Chuck walked by my table. He patted me on the

shoulder. "Great job this year, Ken."

After I recovered from the shock, I admitted to myself that Marissa was a very effective salesperson. She'd shown dedication to AWG over many years, and as I would later learn, Chuck used the award to recognize, not only excellence, but also longevity and commitment.

Would I rather have a plaque or $8,000? I'll take the money.

Chuck's recognition of my hard work motivated me even more. I continued to increase my sales, and the following year, Chuck gave me a $7,000 raise. I made a base salary of $55,000 a year—more than anyone I knew.

I valued other things more than money, like family. But given my background, my earnings humbled me.

I worked for AWG for three years—an accomplishment itself, considering my track record. I probably would've stayed there longer if I didn't keep hearing the call to be an entrepreneur.

chapter twenty-four

Pursuing My Dream

"Some men see things as they are and say why?
I dream things that never were and say, why not?
— George Bernard

I continued to work closely with Mr. Robinson, and I learned as much as I could from him. Not only did he run his four restaurants and do catering, but he also sold his bottled barbeque sauce and rented out other properties. He was respected in the community.

As time went on, I shared with him my dreams for running my own business. "It'll be Ken's Hot Dog Stands."

One day, Mr. Robinson called me. "Ken, come over when you have the chance. There's something I want to talk to you about."

I stopped in to see him on my way home from work.

"You're a sharp young man," he said. "You're going places. I think you have the drive to be a successful business owner."

I smiled. "Thank you, sir." Getting praise from him meant a lot.

"I'm looking at downsizing my restaurant business. You know my restaurant in Woodridge? I'd like to sell it to you."

Whoa! "Really? No kidding?"

"No kidding. I'll sell it to you for $150,000. You can continue to use my name on the restaurant, and you can keep all the equipment and supplies."

His offer seemed too incredible to be true. "Are you sure?"

"Absolutely. I want someone young and energetic to take it over."

For me, $150,000 was a lot of money. But from a business perspective, it was a steal—especially considering I'd get to keep his name and equipment.

As I drove home, I considered ways to come up with the funds. Deidre and I had made plans to build a new home, so that tied up what little equity we had in our townhouse. But I remembered the land in Wildwood, Florida, that Dad's side of the family owned. Grandma and her children held onto it as an investment for some undetermined future use.

Maybe they'll agree to sell some of the land, and we can go into business together. With my extended family's experience in the restaurant business, we had sometimes talked about opening up a family restaurant. *Now's our chance.*

I called Dad in California and told him about the opportunity. It was hard talking long distance about something so important. He'd never heard of Charlie Robinson, and I think I blindsided him with my proposal. "Can you talk to Grandma, Aunt Jean, and Aunt Teanie? Please ask them to consider my proposal."

"Sure, Kenny. But I can't make any promises."

I knew my family might be skeptical at first, but I felt

like the hand of fate had delivered this opportunity. I could close my eyes and visualize running the restaurant. In my visions, I walked around the dining area, greeting customers; I led my employees—inspiring them to reach their fullest potential; and I ordered the best foods and created an enticing menu of dishes. *An opportunity like this doesn't come along very often. This is my time. I'm following my purpose.*

A few days later, I met with Grandma and my aunts at Grandma's house. I explained my proposal. "It's a chance for us to work together."

But they wouldn't listen.

"I'm sorry," Grandma said. She frowned in a sad sort of way. "That land is for security. We can't give it up for something risky."

"We've talked about running a restaurant as a family," I said. "Now we actually have the opp—"

Aunt Jean interrupted. "What are you thinking? There's no way we're touching the land." She crossed her arms and narrowed her eyes. "Don't be taking advantage of us just because you don't have the money."

I stared at the floor. "I'm not trying to take advantage," I mumbled. "It's a solid business. I thought we could do it together."

It was no use.

I stormed out of Grandma's home, got in my car, and slammed the door. *They're scared. They're going to hold onto the land until they die!*

I returned to Mr. Robinson the next day. I looked away from him as I spoke. "I'm sorry. I can't buy your place. Go ahead and sell it to somebody else."

For several weeks, anger consumed me—first directed at my family, and then at myself. One of Chuck's sayings was,

"Success happens when preparation meets opportunity." I wasn't prepared to take the opportunity when it came.

It's my dream, and I need to take responsibility for making it happen.

Fortunately, I loved my job at AWG and that helped me get over my bitterness. But my brush with purchasing a business reaffirmed my dream. I saw it so clearly. Mu'dear had said, "If you can conceive it, you can achieve it." Well, I had no problem conceiving of myself as a business owner. *I'm not just some crazy guy who can't keep a job. I've got the heart of an entrepreneur. It's my purpose in life.* When I was a child, Mu'dear had placed her purpose above keeping a job, and I guess in the end, I was just like her.

My friend Archie and I hung out a lot together. Sometimes, we met for lunch or sat in my car after work and talked. Often, our conversations centered on the potential for starting our own businesses. I still knocked around the idea of Ken's Hot Dog Stands, but that was more a symbol of my dream. In reality, I remained open to any possibility. The more we talked, in fact, the more our ideas gelled around starting a consulting venture together.

Mick and Chuck viewed AWG as a type of consulting business. "Our primary job is to help our customers be successful," Chuck said.

"We could do what Mick and Chuck are doing," I told Archie. "Only we won't sell products. We'll focus on giving advice and helping our clients achieve their goals." Given my varied experience in the food industry, I could help a lot of businesses.

Over several months, we continued to mull over the idea. "We can call ourselves Food Services Solutions," Archie said. It wasn't fancy, but it was a name. And naming an idea is sometimes the first step to making it real.

One day as I drove to my home in Aurora, I noticed a new construction site next to the Fox Valley Mall, located across the street from my townhouse. *That could be a restaurant going up.* Chuck taught me to pay attention to new restaurants and to introduce myself to the owners before they opened.

So for several months, I watched from my family room window as it was built. *That's a busy corner. It's gonna be a popular place.*

Eventually, the construction developed into a beautiful tan stucco building; it looked like a bistro straight out of Venice, Italy. When a banner went up, *Lorenzo's Bistro—Now Hiring,* I made a point to stop by.

As I walked in, I glanced around and whistled. "Whew…" The place looked like it was right out of Greece or Italy. White pillars stood throughout the restaurant, and hand-painted grape vines wrapped around them. It had an open kitchen and granite floors. A huge marble counter separated the kitchen from the dining area, and an oversized vase decorated with red and green peppers and other vegetables sat in the center of the counter.

I introduced myself to the owner and told him I was with AWG. "When you have the time, I'd like to talk to you about some of our products."

His name was Ted Rafokolis, and he spoke with a heavy Greek accent. "I don't mean no disrespect, but I already have food. I'm opening in two weeks, and I don't have enough people. Unless you can help me with people, I can't talk to you now."

"I understand. Here's my card. Feel free to give me a call if you need help with food."

We shook hands, and I left.

When I got home, I immediately wanted to tell Deidre about the restaurant, but she was curled up on the sofa, engrossed in reading a book. That was typical for us after work; I liked to come home and run my mouth, and Dee preferred to grab a good book and relax. One of the many reasons I loved her so much was that she provided a calm counterbalance to my emotional nature.

"You should see the inside of Lorenzo's," I said. "The owner hasn't spared any expense."

"That's nice," Deidre said, her gaze fixed on the page.

"He doesn't need any food, but he does need help with people."

"Well, why don't you help him?" Dee said in a tone that really meant, "Can we talk after I finish this chapter?"

I left her alone and went upstairs to change. But I kept hearing her question in my head, "Why don't you help him?"

Many years earlier, Deidre's uncle had asked me about my plans for the future. Just his few words prompted me to ask Dee to marry me. Now, I felt Dee's words signaling me to action. *This might be a way to get some consulting work.*

I stopped in Lorenzo's the next afternoon. "What kind of help do you need?"

"I need help with service," Ted said.

Well, I'm an expert in managing customer service. "I can do that. I can come in on Friday and Saturday evenings."

"Great. We're training this Friday."

When I came back on Friday, I discovered what he really meant by service—waiting tables. While I listened to the training consultant, I reconsidered my offer to help. *Do I want to wait tables? I'm ready to run a restaurant.*

The trainer demonstrated different techniques for serving customers in a fine dining establishment, such as how to time the delivery of various courses and the formal techniques for serving and removing dishes. I watched, realizing there was a lot I didn't know about waiting tables. That reminded me of something Dad used to say: "In order to have things you've never had before, you've got to be willing to do things you've never done before."

I've never been a server before. What makes me think I can run a restaurant if I've never walked in the shoes of a waiter?

Maybe it was the Holy Spirit, but a gut feeling told me to stick it out at Lorenzo's. *I need to be obedient to this opportunity. Maybe God put those words in Deidre's mouth to push me in this direction.* I decided to stay and wait tables for Ted.

When I told Deidre, she smiled and shook her head. "Here you go, again. Off on another adventure."

"Well, it's your fault," I joked. "You told me to help him."

"I did?"

Deidre never remembered speaking those words that prompted me to help out at Lorenzo's Bistro.

I worked at Lorenzo's on Friday and Saturday evenings. We served fine Italian dishes with a bit of Greek flair. The restaurant exuded elegance: the lights were dimmed; Italian songs played overhead; and a fire blazed from the wood-burning oven. As a server, I wore black pants, a white dress shirt, and a long apron that tied around my waist and ran down to my ankles.

I had a lot to learn about detailed service techniques. But one thing I understood from the start—how to treat customers right. I greeted each customer with a big smile and an enthusiastic attitude. "Hi, I'm Ken, and I'll be your server tonight."

I always talked up the specials. "Tonight we're offering a succulent roasted lamb in a flavorful Marsala wine sauce and an exquisite veal in a lemon sauce."

I studied the wines and which ones to recommend. I learned how to prepare the extra virgin olive oil for the fresh bread, and grate the cheese and grind the pepper over the oil.

Waiting tables at Lorenzo's was like performing on stage; it required perfect timing. I watched to see when my customers finished their appetizers and salads, and when they needed a fresh drink. I used a metal straightedge called a crumb catcher to clear the crumbs off the table, and I tried to do this without my customers even noticing. I gauged whether my patrons were in a hurry or wanted to take their time, and I adjusted accordingly. I became an expert on an array of new foods, like Turtle Soup, Pasta Fazoli, Spumoni, and Canoli.

And I studied how Ted ran the place. In appearance, Ted reminded me of a mob guy. He poofed up his gray hair, wore dark Italian suits, and chewed gum constantly. He could crack a joke, but when it came to his restaurant, he showed an intense perfectionism.

Every night, he stood guard by the marble countertop. He held a towel draped across his arm and inspected every dish the chefs delivered. Sometimes, he added garnish or wiped the edge of the plate with his towel. Each plate was a model in elegant presentation and consistent quality. His eyes beamed with pride as he okayed each dish for the servers to pick up.

I worked at Lorenzo's for the exposure—not the money. But the money wasn't trivial. Most of our customers lived in neighboring Naperville, an affluent suburb of Chicago. The average dinner bill for a party of two was $80. And if a couple purchased a bottle of wine, the bill could go well over $100. I earned as much as $300 from tips on a weekend.

At first Deidre didn't like my working on weekends, but with our plans to build a new home, the extra money came in handy.

In addition to the exposure and money, I simply loved the job. *If I ever lost my job, I could fall back on this and be happy.* Serving others was a family tradition—it ran in my blood.

Ted didn't advertise his restaurant, but word spread nonetheless. Within two months, long lines for seating formed every weekend evening. Ted impressed me with how he channeled his commitment for excellence into a thriving enterprise.

As the business grew, some customers returned again and again. One time, an African-American couple entered the restaurant and approached the hostess. The man was stocky and wore a blue suit, and he pointed at me. A few minutes later, the hostess told me the man had requested me as his server; he was willing to wait longer until one of my tables opened up.

When they got seated, the gentleman introduced himself and his wife. "My name's Eric and this is my wife Edie. We really appreciated the great service you gave us last time."

I didn't remember serving them before, but apparently

I'd done something right.

Eric and his wife returned about every other Friday, and each time, they requested one of my tables. His wife never talked to me, but Eric talked a lot. He told me about his work as a director with United Parcel Service and about his family.

And I told him about my family—about Deidre, my son Austin, and the baby on the way.

One time he asked, "You don't do this for a living, do you?"

I don't know why he asked me that, but I replied honestly. "No. I work for a food broker. I just work here on the weekends."

That prompted me to share my work background and my dream. I got excited and talked fast. "I'm really an entrepreneur at heart. I'm helping Ted for a while and learning from him. My business will either be Ken's Hot Dog Stands or Food Services Solutions."

Edie ignored me and gazed out the window as I spoke.

I don't think she likes me. Maybe she thinks I talk too much.

But Eric looked me in the eyes and nodded. "That's great," he said. "I know it'll happen for you."

Every time they returned, Eric talked to me about my dream.

"Thank you for showing so much interest," I said.

Archie and I continued to brainstorm about Food Services Solutions. "Why don't we search for companies looking to hire people like us?" I said. "We can offer our consulting services, instead. The business ads in the paper might have something."

One Sunday morning, I spotted an ad from the McDonald's Corporation in the *Chicago Tribune*. I read the top part of the ad. Printed in big block letters, it read: "Come have continental breakfast with McDonald's upper management this Saturday."

I didn't read the rest of the ad. *I'm there.*

I called Archie and told him I'd attend the breakfast. "If we get them as a client, it'll be over. Everyone'll want to work with us."

Saturday morning, I put on my suit and drove to the McDonald's corporate headquarters. The event would change my life. But in a way I never expected.

chapter twenty-five

From Catastrophe to Opportunity

*"Success consist of getting up just one
more time than you fall." — Oliver Goldsmith*

I entered a lobby at the McDonald's corporate
headquarters, and a woman in a brown business
suit greeted me. She wore a white nametag
with the golden arches emblem on it. "How're you doing?
Welcome to the open house."

Open house? I stopped walking in. "I thought this was
a breakfast."

"Yes, we have coffee, Danish and other items down this
way." She pointed to her left. Tables containing brochures and
other information filled the room, and decorative streamers
hung from the ceilings.

This is a job fair!

"Please check out all our tables," the woman said.
"There's plenty of information on our career opportunities."

I walked into the room—but only for a moment to
gather my thoughts. *What am I doing here? I've got a great job. I
don't need a job fair.* As I turned to leave, a glossy McDonald's

brochure caught my attention. *I might as well grab a brochure and do some research.*

I picked up the brochure and thumbed through it. *This company's huge. I don't know anything about McDonald's except burgers and fries.*

Thinking I needed to learn more about the organization, I decided to stay for a few minutes. I milled around the room with other guests, picked up more flyers, and watched an informational video. I avoided eye contact with people. *I might run into somebody I know.*

Again I considered leaving, but this time a man ushered everyone into a nearby auditorium. "Some of our management representatives will be giving a presentation."

Maybe I can meet the executives I originally thought I could talk with.

The crowd made its way into the auditorium, and I followed. A panel of people was seated on the stage; and I found a chair about twenty rows back. After everyone took a seat, a man strode into the auditorium, followed by an entourage of five people. A security guard at the two exits closed the doors and stood in front of them.

A woman approached the podium. "We ask that everyone remain seated during the presentations. You'll have an opportunity to meet the speakers afterward."

There's no way out now. I later learned that the man who had entered was the CEO, and that the company followed strict security procedures wherever he went—hence, the guards at the doors and the request to remain seated.

Another woman stepped to the podium. "Hello. My name's Rosanna, and I'm originally from Mexico. I started with McDonald's eight years ago as a crew member, and now I'm a store manager." Rosanna talked for about five minutes, telling the audience how McDonald's had helped her advance and given her opportunities unavailable at other companies.

After Rosanna, a supervisor spoke. He had also started on a crew and now was responsible for five stores. After him, another gentleman came up to talk. He was an operations manager, and again his story was similar to the previous two.

As the people presented their stories, I only half listened. Instead, I focused more on reading the information I'd picked up from the tables.

When the operations manager finished, I glanced up and saw an African-American woman approach the podium. *Oh, no! She looks familiar.* I looked at the two exit doors. The guards still blocked them.

I have to get out of here. But I couldn't. My skin grew hot and my heart pounded.

I didn't know anyone who worked for McDonald's, but I was sure I knew her. *Maybe she's with a supplier. She probably works for Simplot!*

I slumped down in my chair and put my hand to my forehead, shielding my eyes from view. *She's going to see me and tell AWG. I'm gonna get fired.*

I didn't hear a word she said. I just kept scoping out those doors and trying to figure out how to get free. Sweat dripped down the side of my face, and I squirmed in my seat. Finally, the lady sat down, and a vice president got up to talk. After him, the CEO spoke. He might as well have talked in a foreign language. All I could think about was how on earth I'd explain my presence at a McDonald's job fair.

After the CEO finished, he and his entourage exited the auditorium. As the other speakers left, the hostess announced that the panel members would wait outside the doors to shake hands and answer any questions. I turned away as the familiar woman walked by my row.

While the crowd filed out, I tried to sneak around the receiving line, but there was no room. *Here you go, getting yourself into another mess. Lord, have mercy on me.*

The management team had formed a line in the gathering area immediately outside the door. As we made our way forward, I shook hands with Rosanna and the two men that followed her.

I approached the woman that I'd recognized and stared at the floor. My heart raced faster. I shook her hand and tried to proceed quickly.

But she held firm to my hand. "I know you," she said, refusing to let go.

"No, I don't think so." I'm sure she felt the sweat on my palm.

"Yes, I definitely know you from somewhere."

I looked up at her. "No, ma'am. I'm sorry. I really don't think so."

Her eyes opened a little wider, and she smiled. "Lorenzo's," she said in a tone of recognition. "You're the waiter from Lorenzo's. Ken's your name."

Huh?

Still holding my hand, she turned toward some of the people around her. "Gentlemen, lock the doors."

Oh, dear God. I'm done for! Why's she locking the doors? I searched my memory and couldn't remember her from Lorenzo's. *I'm trapped.*

She asked me to stand aside and said she'd get back with me in a minute. There was no reason to run now. She'd found me out.

After the receiving line filtered out, she walked over to

me, followed by two men. Her hair was well styled, and her nails manicured. She wore a pair of stylish wire rim glasses and a sharp-looking blue suit. I tried to place her, but my panicked mind couldn't think straight.

"Gentlemen," she said to the two men. "Eric and I've been eating at this restaurant in Naperville, and this gentleman right here has been serving us."

Ohhh…Edie. It's Eric's wife, Edie.

"His level of professionalism is exceptional," she said. "The quality of his service is the best I've ever seen. He makes us feel special every time we enter that restaurant."

Wow. She's never talked to me. I thought she didn't like me.

"Not only that, he has a vision for his life. He knows what he wants to do."

She has been listening to me.

"The way Eric and I feel every time we go to Lorenzo's— that's the way we want our customers to feel. That's our vision for the future of McDonald's."

I sighed and smiled. Her praise resurrected me. She really did work for McDonald's, and I wasn't going to get fired. She even liked me. *I'm back in the game.*

"Thank you," I said. "I'm honored you feel that way." I stood up straighter and looked her in the eye. "That's why I'm here—because of my vision. I didn't come here for a job fair. I didn't even know it was a job fair."

I turned toward the men. "You see, my friend Archie and I have a business called Food Services Solutions. I came here to meet the upper management and suggest that you hire us as consultants. We can help make your vision come to fruition."

The men smiled slyly.

Edie looked at them. "See what I mean, gentleman? Do you feel his zeal?"

I smiled at her. "So, who do I talk to? Which one of you makes the decisions?"

Edie chuckled. "We all do." She thanked the men for coming over and asked me to sit with her for a minute.

We took a seat on a leather sofa. "Listen," she said. "You don't know me very well, and I don't know you. But I see your passion, and I remember your vision. I got a feeling about you. In five years, you could be where I am—and it took me twenty years to get here."

"I'm flattered, but I'm not trying to be where you are." I shifted in my seat and faced her directly. "I've got a great job now, but I'm an entrepreneur. I want you to hire me as a consultant."

"I understand that. But think about it anyway and give me a call." She handed me a white business card with the golden arches emblem. It read: "Edie Waddell, District Manager, Warrenville, Illinois." Warrenville was just down the road from my house.

She shook my hand. "You can trust me, Ken." And then she stood up and walked away.

As soon as I got in my car, I called Archie. "They weren't interested in any consulting. Instead, they want to hire me."

"For what?"

"I don't have a clue. It's crazy."

When I arrived home, I pulled out the business card, set it on my desk, and stared at it. *I should pitch this thing. I've already done fast food.* But I let it sit there for a while.

I talked to Deidre as she folded clothes.

"You know," she said. "I used to drive past their

headquarters on the way to work each day. I remember driving by once and looking at their campus. All of a sudden, something came over me. I got this strange sense of comfort—peace, really—driving by the place. The feeling didn't make sense, but I never forgot it."

She touched my arm. "I'm not telling you what to do, but maybe you should consider this."

Later that evening, Archie called. I chuckled again at the idea of McDonald's wanting to hire me.

"I don't know why you think it's funny," he said. "I know you. You'll go in that company and work your way up quickly. You'll own three McDonald's in three years."

I laughed. "Yeah, right. Now you're crazy."

"I'm okay with it. You should talk to them."

After I got off, I noticed the McDonald's ad sitting on my desk. At the top, it read: "Come have continental breakfast with McDonald's upper management this Saturday." That was the part I'd seen. But underneath, it read: "A Career Open House."

I'd never read that. If I had, I would've known it was a job fair, and I wouldn't have gone. *Maybe I wasn't supposed to know.*

The next week, Archie and I were scheduled to attend a tradeshow. He picked me up early in the morning, and we drove to the show. Along the way, he pulled into a McDonald's drive-thru to get breakfast. McDonald's had just come out with their breakfast bagels, and he wanted to try one.

As Archie ordered, I looked into the pickup window and saw a gray-haired, middle-aged man in a shirt and tie. He hurriedly filled the orders for his crew at the registers. He reminded me a bit of Steve Wilt, the owner of the Schaumburg Wendy's where I'd worked for three months.

Maybe I could own a McDonald's. Now may be the time to stick my neck out again and see what happens.

That evening I picked Edie's business card off the desk and gave her a call. We met a week later at her Warrenville office.

"I have a plan for my district," she said. "And I need some out-of-the-box thinkers to get us to the next level."

She called someone on the phone and asked the person to come to her office. After she hung up, she looked back at me. "I'm a Ken Brown fan. But we work as a team here, and I need to include somebody else in this decision if this plan's going to work." She explained that people normally didn't come into McDonald's management from off the street. Everyone had worked his or her way up from a crew position.

A Caucasian man entered the room and smiled warmly. His name was Mike Flores, and he also managed a district.

I reviewed my background with him, and he was impressed. "So, Ken, where do you see yourself in five years?"

I looked out the window behind him and watched the cars zoom by on the expressway. Almost every interviewer I'd ever talked with asked that question. Up until now, I told people what they wanted to hear—that I wanted to move up the ranks of their company. *Now I've got nothing to lose. I might as well be truthful.*

"To be honest, in five years I won't be at McDonald's. I've got an entrepreneurial spirit, and I'm going to own a business. It's going to be Ken's Hot Dog Stands."

Mike laughed. "I like that."

"But I guarantee that if you hire me, I'll give you

excellence. And when I depart, I'll leave you wanting more."

He smiled. "Could you start your restaurant in three years?"

"Sir, I could do it tomorrow if I had the money."

He laughed again and nodded at Edie. "I like this guy."

They both left for a moment, and then Edie came back. "Okay, we're going to put together an offer. I've got a vision for you. If you accept, then I'll put you on a fast track training program. I'll work with our Human Resources Department to set it up."

The next day Edie called and offered me a compensation package totaling $80,000—an unbelievable amount of money. "I'm taking a chance, but if you live up to your passion, then you'll do great. You'll have to become an expert on our operations. You'll need to be as knowledgeable as our long-time employees."

"And one more thing," she said, "I'm paying enough to cover your Lorenzo's income. If you accept the job, you'll be here for a purpose. I can't have you working another job."

I didn't understand completely the purpose she referred to. But she sounded determined, and that gave me confidence in her plan.

I took a few days to think it over. Taking the job would require giving up a lot. I loved working at Lorenzo's, and I loved working at AWG. More important, I loved Chuck. He was a mentor and a great role model. I'd worked at AWG for three-and-a-half years, and I knew I had a job with them until I quit or died.

My future was certain with them, and in a strange way, that made me uncomfortable. Knowing God cared for me through the evictions and periods of unemployment had taught me to accept—even embrace—uncertainty.

I was torn. At night, I tossed and turned. During the day, I consulted with friends, my parents, and especially my wife.

Deidre advised me to pray about it. "I trust that God will lead you to the right decision."

I did pray. *Why was this put before me, Lord? Which way should I choose?*

I thought about the chain of events that had led up to this point: making the strange decision to work at Lorenzo's, meeting and befriending Eric Waddell, seeing the McDonald's ad but not reading about the job fair, and my failure to avoid Edie at the job fair. The events had unfolded like somebody's plan.

An executive with McDonald's sees something in me. I'll be making more money and working close to home.

The more I thought about it, the more excited I got. *I'm going to do it.*

I immediately felt at peace. That peace, I believe, was God's answer to my prayers.

But now I had to tell Chuck.

chapter twenty-six

Years Into Months at McDonald's

"So teach us to number our days, that we may apply our hearts unto wisdom." — Psalm 90:12

For a few days after accepting the McDonald's job, I wasn't man enough to talk to Chuck. I felt I'd betrayed him. I also worried that he wouldn't understand why I was leaving. *He's going to think I went shopping for another job.*

But I couldn't avoid the conversation forever. So, I worked up the nerve and asked to meet him for breakfast. I felt too disloyal to go to the office.

We met at a Greek restaurant in Des Plaines, halfway between Vernon Hills and my home in Aurora. I got there first, and then Chuck walked in and sat down at my table. "You're leaving, aren't you?"

Dang. "Why do you say that?"

"I just know. I could tell by the tone in your voice."

"Let me explain it."

He let out a deep sigh and leaned back in his chair. "Fine. Lay your cards on the table." He looked hard at me.

I told him the job was with McDonald's, and that a district manager was putting me through a fast track program. "She said I could be where she is in five years, and it took her twenty years to get there."

Chuck's face softened as I spoke. After I finished, he said, "Well, it sounds like a great opportunity, and I'm excited for you. I hate to see you go—you're part of the family. But go with our blessings."

Whew! I exhaled loudly. "Thank you. You don't know how much that means to me."

"I'll let Mick and the group know."

Later that day, I received a call from Mick. "I want to meet with you. Can you come in the office?"

"Sure." Since Chuck had given me his blessing, I didn't mind going there. I sat down in Mick's office and spotted his McDonald's hard hat sitting on a shelf. He asked me about the job offer, and I filled him in on the details.

"I spent a lot of time working with McDonald's while I was with Otto and Sons," he said. "Even as a supplier, you're still part of McFamily." He smiled. "If you were leaving to go anywhere else, I'd say you were crazy. McDonald's is a classy organization. You're going to be successful there."

"Thank you, sir." *This must be a sign I'm doing the right thing.*

After we finished talking, he walked me out of his office and announced my departure to the rest of the group. Everyone congratulated me and showed genuine excitement for my opportunity. I never forgot how AWG let me go with dignity and their blessing.

Ted at Lorenzo's reacted the same way. "It's a great company. I own stock in McDonald's. Make sure I make some money on my investment, okay?"

On my first day at McDonald's, I met with a man from Human Resources. "Oh yes, Ken Brown. I heard about you," he said, crossing his arms over his chest. There was a snide tone in his voice. "You're Edie's boy, aren't you?" I didn't like being called anybody's boy. I'd worked hard to chart my own path. I'd built my own identity.

He thumbed through some papers on his desk. "She must like you. She's got quite a plan laid out. Beats me how you'll finish this in six months. It takes most of us twenty years to get this far." He flipped hard through the papers. "It's going to take a lot of time on your part. A lot of commitment."

"I'm ready," I said. "I'm committed."

Edie assigned me to a store in Schaumburg—the same town where I'd worked for Steve Wilt, the Wendy's franchise owner. "You'll shadow the manager for two months and learn from him," she said.

The Schaumburg store was an old restaurant in a high volume location. It had a diverse crew, made up of African-Americans, Caucasians, and Hispanics. I especially enjoyed working with the Hispanic employees; they hustled and responded well to my energetic style.

Several times, I took time off from the store to attend a multi-day McDonald's management workshop. I took the Basic Shift Management class and sailed through it. Most people attended one class every year or two, but I went about every third week. After Basic Shift Management, I took Advanced Shift Management. Then I took other courses such as Effective People Management.

Sometimes the HR Department forgot to register me for a scheduled workshop. I didn't think their forgetfulness was accidental. I'd have to call and hound them. "I'm supposed to be in this class." Only through my persistence did I stay on pace.

In the classes, people occasionally made spiteful comments about the track I was on. "You haven't done your time at McDonald's," one guy told me. "You shouldn't be in this class yet." He saw I had a company car and that frustrated him even more.

"You're right," I said. "I haven't done my time at McDonald's, and I respect you because you've given your commitment to this company for twenty years. But I've given my commitment to the entire food service industry. So nothing is different. Commitment is commitment; we both add value. There's more than one way to achieve a goal."

I didn't know McDonald's as well as the others. But I knew people. And I knew food. During class discussions, other people talked about their McDonald's experiences, but I shared a variety of industry experiences. My classmates eventually respected me for my knowledge. At the end of each workshop, the students voted for the best class contributor. In all but one class, they voted me that honor.

After two months, Edie called again. "I've got another project I want to put you on. We just opened our 25,000[th] restaurant. It's on the south side, at 26th and Indiana. I want you to go over there and do your thing—use your expertise and passion to help them out."

The store had opened two weeks prior to my assignment, and they were still working out the kinks. It was a franchise store—owned by Mr. and Mrs. Porter. Mr. Porter had been a postmaster in Chicago before he started the restaurant.

The place was located in an area called Bronzeville, which had a rich jazz history. It was the nicest McDonald's I'd ever been in. A jazz theme ran throughout the restaurant. They piped in jazz music, and on Friday nights, brought in live jazz performers. In the lobby, a glass case displayed a saxophone and a trumpet, along with photographs of Dizzy Gillespie and Duke Ellington and other memorabilia. Pendulum lighting hung over the tables, and slate tiles covered the floor. The employees wore white button-down shirts and ties with jazz designs on them. The restaurant even had its own logo: the golden arches with a piano and saxophone worked into it.

As the 25,000th store, it enjoyed a high profile. Customers came from miles around to see it. McDonald's corporate staff and out-of-town employees frequently stopped by. Even Oprah Winfrey previewed the restaurant on her television show.

It was in the inner city but just down the road from the new police headquarters, so it was in a good location. The store was Edie's baby. She wanted to make it special and successful, so she committed additional resources to getting the operation off the ground.

She'd already assigned two McDonald's consultants to work there. The consultants worked directly with the Porters, but I jumped in and mixed it up with the crew. I rolled up my sleeves and worked the grill or the drive-thru or wherever I could demonstrate how to do things. I joked around with the workers and encouraged them. I was in my element.

As a team, everyone worked hard and put in a lot of hours. The Porters, in particular, poured their energy into ensuring their place was a success. After two months, the place ran smoothly.

"I'm really proud of you," I told Mr. and Mrs. Porter.

"I'd love to do this myself someday."

The Porters didn't have prior restaurant experience, but they had money. My situation was the opposite. *If I put in my time at McDonald's and save my income, maybe my time will come.*

After Bronzeville, Edie assigned me to a store in Warrenville. "It's not living up to its potential. I want you to go in there and help turn things around."

The Warrenville manager, Jason, through a mutual agreement with McDonald's, had recently stepped down as a supervisor and returned to the store level. But now he was *camping.* He still made supervisor pay and drove a company car, but he didn't take an active role in leading his restaurant. He didn't engage the crew or work with them. He got angry a lot and vented his frustration on his employees. Crew morale was low.

Despite its location on a main thoroughfare, the store performed poorly. "Warrenville is an old area," Jason said. "People around here aren't interested in fast food."

That's ridiculous. In reality, he didn't serve his customers with excellence, so people didn't want to eat there. McDonald's had recently remodeled the place. It looked nice, but a face-lift only went so far. *This place needs heart surgery.*

After six months with McDonald's, I finished most of my training. Only one thing remained: Hamburger University. The name sounded silly, but Hamburger U was the key training event within the McDonald's Corporation. It was a week-long, intensive school, usually reserved for supervisors, or managers who'd worked in their positions for at least two years.

About two hundred people attended along with me. My fellow classmates came from all over the world, including Great Britain, Germany, France, Hong Kong, China, and Africa. Many people waited most of their careers to go to HU. If people passed the school, then they received an actual diploma with a bachelor degree in Hamburgerology. For some of them, it was the only degree they'd ever received.

Because of the program's significance, classmates again expressed frustration and bewilderment over my fast track schedule. But I stayed focused on my mission, and for the most part, I didn't let it get to me. *I'll show them I'm worthy.*

At HU, we used textbooks, sat in lecture halls, and learned from professors. They gave us quizzes and exams every day and posted our scores by Social Security Number outside the classrooms—just like at college. If we missed less than ten points during the entire week, the school honored us with placement on the dean's list.

During the evenings, people went sightseeing downtown, especially those who were from other countries, but I stayed in my hotel room and studied. I was from Chicago; I didn't need to sightsee. Plus, I wanted to be on that dean's list.

At the end of the week, McDonald's threw a fancy dinner banquet to celebrate our graduation. A speaker rose to announce those people who'd made the dean's list. The first name he read was, "Ken Brown."

I jumped up from my chair. "Yeah! All right!"

The people at my table clapped and cheered.

Lord, have mercy. It felt great. I'd proven my worth.

The next Monday, I returned to work at the Warrenville

store. Upon my arrival, I learned that Jason had quit. The store was mine.

PART 3 —
BUILT TO SERVE

chapter twenty-seven

A PROVEN TRACK RECORD

"Reputation is what you are suppose to be: character is what you are." — Unknown

"I know you're Edie's special project," said Rich Koopman, the Operations Manager for my group. He was a muscular, executive-looking guy, and almost a foot taller than me. He grabbed my shoulder when he talked to me. "She's gotten you this far. Now let's see what you can do."

Rich reminded me of some of the tough neighborhood kids I encountered growing up. Every time we moved, I had to gain their respect to be accepted. Now, I committed myself once again to proving my worth.

It's finally time for some heart surgery in Warrenville. During my first two weeks, I sat down with every employee. "If I were to grade our store right now, I'd give us an F," I told them. "But I want you to be part of the solution. What would it take for us to be an A?"

They offered plenty of suggestions, and I took notes on everything they said: "We don't have any teamwork."

"We're short-staffed." "Equipment breaks down too often." "The store's always filthy."

I decided that keeping the store clean was the best place to start. A restaurant's cleanliness often motivates employees to take more pride in their job. I sat down with José, our maintenance and cleaning man and asked him what we could do. José had worked for McDonald's a long time, and he was frustrated. He dressed sloppy—his shirttail always hung out, and grease spots blotted his pants. He rarely smiled.

"I don't have all the equipment I need," he said. "And we're so short-staffed, that half the time, I do other people's jobs and not mine."

I promised to fully dedicate him to maintenance and cleaning and to provide the supplies he needed. "In exchange," I said, "I want you coming to work looking the way I want the store to look—clean and polished."

José agreed. He tested me, though. Almost every day for a week, he brought me a new list of things he needed: mops, buckets, squeegees, new uniforms, and a loose jacket for working in the cooler.

I got him everything. I needed an ally, and José responded. He cleaned the bathrooms and windows, scrubbed the floors, and manicured the lawns. The place sparkled. He filtered the oil and maintained the equipment in its best working order.

The place took on a new appearance, and the crew responded with more pride in their work. In the past, when a crewmember made a mess, they might not have cleaned it up. Now, they cleaned it up right away. Even the speed with which they worked and how they treated customers improved. I also recruited new employees, and with full crews, we reduced our customer service times even more.

But as I observed the crew, one thing still bothered me—their uniforms. They wore blue polo shirts that looked a bit ragged. *Polo shirts are for golf, not restaurants.* I remembered the dress shirts and ties the crew wore at the Porter's jazz-themed store. So, I bought my crew the same white shirts, as well as black ties and visors. The crew looked great. They seemed to smile more and stand up straighter.

Many employees continued to give me ideas for improvements. I listened to everything they said and followed their advice whenever it was appropriate. At a minimum, they knew they had a manager who respected them.

Sales picked up. The additional staff, uniforms, and maintenance supplies cost money, but the increased revenues and profits paid for the investment.

I continued to institute changes. I initiated an Adopt-an-Equipment Program. Each crewmember agreed to adopt a part of the kitchen and ensure it was kept in good working order. I drew up adoption certificates and had each person sign them. An example would be: "I, Miguel Chavez, hereby agree I will duly adopt the grill. I promise to keep it maintained and treat it like my baby." I then affixed each of the certificates to the appropriate piece of equipment, such as the grills, fryers, shake machine, and coffee machines.

In the dining room, two old televisions hung from the ceiling. They didn't work and were covered with dust. I replaced them, and they seemed to attract more customers.

Also, an old magazine rack sat empty in the lobby. Instead of using it again for magazines, I asked Deidre for some children's books. She was still a schoolteacher and had plenty of leftover books. Dee had a great little reading nook in her classroom, so I copied that idea and bought a throw rug and some beanbag chairs from Wal-Mart. The Warrenville store became the first McDonald's I knew of that offered a children's reading area.

On a continual basis, McDonald's hired mystery shoppers to come into each restaurant and pose as customers. They rated us on how well we served them and the quality of our food. Then they'd send us reports that evaluated how well we did. I hung all the reports on a bulletin board in the back. I praised our crew when we excelled and pointed out the areas where we needed improvement.

Like I always had, I rolled up my sleeves and worked side-by-side with the crew whenever help was needed. I came in on weekends and sometimes closed the store at nights with them. My assistant managers knew they could call me at home any time.

One Friday while I helped close, I glanced at the main road outside the store. A steady flow of traffic still crossed in front of us. That gave me another idea. "I'm going to go 24 hours," I told Rich Koopman. "We're on a main drag, and there's a lot of traffic out there on weekend nights."

I got one of the assistant managers and a couple of the crewmembers on board with the plan. We stayed open all night on Fridays and Saturdays, and our sales increased even more.

Over three months, we saw a double-digit growth in revenues compared to the previous year. I was proud of the assistant managers and my entire crew. We'd worked together to turn the Warrenville restaurant from an F store to an A store.

About that time, I received a voicemail that was broadcast to all the management in the region. It was from

Phil Gray. "I'd like to announce that Edie Waddell has been promoted to Regional Vice President for the Michigan Region. Edie has been with McDonald's for twenty-seven years and has a proven track record of leadership and excellence. She'll be a vital asset to her new region."

I was thrilled for her. She deserved the promotion. I'd proven myself at Bronzeville and Warrenville, so I didn't worry that her departure would negatively impact my career. I could set my own course.

At her going away party, I hugged her and thanked her for the opportunity she'd given me.

"I've heard great things about you," she said. "I'm proud of you."

She asked how far along I was in my training, and I told her I'd completed all my classes and Hamburger University.

"Then you're ready to supervise."

"Absolutely."

"Okay, I'm going to make that happen."

A few weeks later, Rich came to the store to meet with me. It was a warm, sunny day, and José stood outside hosing down the sidewalks. Rich and I sat at a table and watched the large lunchtime crowd fill up the lobby. I felt like a proud papa.

Rich glanced at me and shook his head. "They're taking you from me. I hate to let you go—the place won't be the same without you."

"I'm going somewhere else? Where?"

"You're being promoted."

He smiled and shook my hand firmly. "Congratulations. You deserve it."

I'm not sure what made me more proud, watching my crew achieve success or winning Rich's respect.

The next day, I received another regional voicemail. It was from the HR Department. "We would like to announce that Ken Brown has been promoted to Supervisor." They skipped the usual part about years of service with McDonald's. "He has a proven track record with innovation and increasing sales."

I was grateful to Edie for everything she did. Yes, I'd worked hard and committed myself to excellence, but I knew my rapid advancement within McDonald's wouldn't have happened without her.

As a supervisor, I had responsibility over four stores: Downers Grove East, Downers Grove West, Lisle, and Westmont. My operations manager was Curt Oxyer, and he was an out-of-the box thinker like Edie. We hit it off. He did things differently and allowed me to do things differently. He ran his stores efficiently and achieved a high sales rate. People respected him.

Four store managers, twenty assistant managers, and around two hundred crew reported to me. The store managers were all women—three Hispanic and one Caucasian—and very hard workers. They'd worked at McDonald's for a long time and performed their jobs extremely well, so I tried to impart my non-McDonald's experience to help round out their knowledge. I also encouraged them to continue growing in their careers. "My job is to help you reach your goals."

One of the mangers in particular, Rosita, aspired to be a supervisor. I worked with her to develop the needed skills, and I spread the word about her at our regional office. Six months later, she was promoted to supervisor.

I continued to engage the crews. I knew just about all their names and worked closely with them. A supervisor's job was normally Monday through Friday, but I stopped in the stores on weekends or closed with them late at night.

Although I spent time at the stores, my office was located at the regional headquarters. I got to know everyone there, from the secretaries up to the Regional Vice President, Phil Gray. I came in the office a lot on Saturdays and sometimes Phil also stopped in. He always walked by my office. "How are the stores doing?" he'd ask. I enjoyed getting to know him on a more personal level.

At home, my two children, Austin and Bradley, were now four and two years old. We'd moved into a single-family house in a new subdivision. The house was a dream come true. It was a four-bedroom home, 3,200 square feet, with an unfinished basement. It had a first floor office, oak floors, and a laundry room attached to the garage.

As the movers brought our belongings into the new home, I remembered those moves I'd made as a child, with one bag of clothes slung over my shoulder. *Thank you, Lord, for delivering me this far.*

One Saturday while I was in the office, Phil stopped by. "I saw Edie at a meeting last week."

"That's great. I hope she's doing well."

"Well, you can find out yourself," he said and then smiled. "She wants to talk to you. Here's her number."

I figured she just wanted to see how I was doing, so I didn't call her for several days.

One evening at home, I got around to phoning her.

My boys were playing upstairs, so I took the phone into the basement.

"I heard things are going well for you," she said.

"I couldn't be happier." I meant it. Things were perfect: I enjoyed my job; I had a wonderful family; and now I had a new home.

"Listen, I talked to Phil about you. We talked about you relocating to Michigan."

"What?"

Edie shared some of the things she was trying to do in Detroit, but I didn't listen very well. My thoughts ran wild. In following my ambitions over the years, I'd never considered moving out of Chicago for a job. Yes, I'd made it out of the inner city, but the Chicago area was my home. Most of my family and friends lived there. I knew Deidre never wanted to leave. I'd never understood how people uprooted their families for just a job.

After all Edie's done for me, how do I tell her no.

She kept talking. "Do you remember telling me you wanted to become an owner?"

"Yeah. I still want to."

"Well, I watched the way you handled those restaurants—Warrenville in particular. The sales were incredible, not to mention the quality and the cleanliness. Now you're doing that with four stores. Which made me think, if you did that with those stores, what would you do with your own?"

Where's she going with this?

"I need some operationally sound owner/operators in Detroit, and I want you to be part of my plan to change things."

"I'm not sure what you mean. I don't exactly have the

money to buy a store."

"Don't worry about that right now. Can you come up to Detroit to meet with me?"

I had no idea where things were headed. I didn't understand how she could be talking about my owning a store. But it was a dream of mine, and I had to at least see what it was all about.

"Sure," I said. "I'd be glad to."

chapter twenty-eight

Two Stores, Three Million Dollars, and A Whole Lot of Faith

"Now unto him that is able to do exceedingly abundantly above all that we ask or think, according to the power that worketh in us." — Ephesians 3:20

I went into the office and discovered a manila envelope, maybe half an inch thick, sitting on my desk. I opened it up and peeked inside. The top page was titled: Franchise Application. I pulled it out and looked it over; it asked for financial information such as assets and liabilities. *I don't have any assets and liabilities.*

I jammed the application back in the envelope and dropped it on the desk. *Whoa, she's serious. This is crazy.*

Later that night, I brought the packet home and laid it on the kitchen counter. Deidre stood nearby chopping onions. "Dee, there's something I need to talk to you about. I need you to look over this packet, but first I need to tell you what's going on." She continued working while I talked. "I had a conversation with Edie. She wants me to move to Michigan and—"

"Hold it right there, Mr. Cowboy." Deidre stopped cutting and stared at me. "We're not going anywhere. That's where your adventures stop."

"Wait a second, Dee. She wants me to be an owner."

"What are you talking about, Kenny? How you gonna own a McDonald's? Where you gonna get the money from?"

"I don't know. I don't know that yet."

"We just built this house. We just decorated it. Everyone we know is in Chicago." She shook her head. "You're out of your mind." She'd never reacted so strongly to one of my opportunities before, but I'd never asked so much of her, either.

I picked up the envelope. "Just look at this packet. It's a franchise application that was…"

Deidre exhaled and went back to chopping.

She didn't want to hear anymore. "Tell you what. I want you to pray about this for a few days, and then we'll talk about it. I won't touch the application unless you tell me it's a go. I'll just tell Edie no—I don't have a problem doing that."

I had long dreamed of owning a restaurant, but I loved Deidre more than my dream. If I was supposed to be an entrepreneur, God would present another opportunity. I was only thirty-five years old. *There'll be other chances.*

A few nights later as we got into bed, Deidre started asking questions. "Tell me more about this," she said. "We'll actually be owners?"

"Yes. I won't work at a McDonald's store any longer; I'll own it. We'll own it. Edie's the vice president up there. She sees something in me and thinks I can be successful."

Dee asked more questions, and I did my best to answer, even though I didn't know many of the details.

"Okay," she said. "Let's fill out the application."

Yes! I leaned over and kissed her. "What made you change your mind?"

"Well, I've been praying about it. And yesterday I was reading a book by T. D. Jakes called *Maximize the Moment.* I came across a passage that really resonated with me. Basically, he said that when God is ready for us to move, we've got to move. He can't bless us where we are."

Thank you, T. D. Jakes!

The next night, Deidre and I completed the application form. We couldn't fill in most of the blanks; we had some equity in the house, Deidre's small 401k, and maybe $1,000 in the bank. Nothing more.

The next time I went into the office, I laid the application on the desk of George Gudgeon—the director of finance for the Chicago Region. *Oh well, this process might at least give me a glimpse of what the future could hold. I can't imagine qualifying for a store right now.*

Two days later, George poked his head in my office. "Oh, by the way, Ken. It's a go." He gave me the thumbs-up sign.

"It's a go?"

"Yeah, your credit checked out. We can do the deal."

"Deal?" I didn't mean to sound stupid, but I couldn't figure out how they were making it work.

Later that day, I received a phone call from John Parlow of the Michigan Region. "Edie asked me to give you a call. She wants you to come to Michigan and tour some of our stores—see which ones you might be interested in."

"Which ones? Plural?"

"She can explain more about the deal when you get here."

When I got to Detroit, Edie wasn't there. Instead, I met with Dee Johnson, the McDonald's controller for Michigan. "I can give you some information on the region." He unloaded a ton of information on me, such as regional financial figures, customer demographics, and owner profiles. Most of it was over my head, but I kept nodding like I knew what he was talking about.

Then he asked questions. "Who's in your organization?"

"Organization?"

"Yeah, your bookkeeper, your tax accountant, your administrative assistant, and so on."

"Um, I'm working on that."

"Do you have a pro forma?"

I knew that a pro forma was some type of financial document, but that was all I knew. "Uh, not yet."

"Okay, well, you need to get one together."

I'm in over my head. I'm gonna end up saying something foolish. I tapped my foot nervously as I tried to give a serious, knowing look.

Then John Parlow took me on a tour. We visited six stores. He gave a rundown on each restaurant: information on its history, whether it was an owner/operator or company store, and area demographics.

After each visit, I tried to think of things to ask. "Why are they selling?" Or, "What do you think of their customer base?"

As he answered my questions, I nodded and tried to understand. For the most part, however, I ran on faith. I was riding a wild roller coaster, and I had no idea where it was going. But God had delivered me this far, so I did my best to trust him.

Before I headed home, Dee Johnson touched base with me one more time. "I'm working on your deal. I still have some things to complete, and then Edie will need to approve it. So hang tight, okay?"

"Okay." I didn't know what else to say. What else could I say? I didn't even understand exactly what he meant by a deal.

When I returned to Warrenville, I received a voicemail from Edie. "I'm sorry I missed you," she said. "I had to go out of town. But we're putting the finishing touches on the deal. We'll have it ready soon. We want to get this thing started by the first of May."

That's only one month away!

Later that day, Phil Gray called me into his office. He'd often stopped by to chat with me, but he'd never summoned me into his office before.

I took a seat, and he closed the door.

"I know what you've been working on with Edie."

Uh-oh. I'm in trouble.

"I just want to wish you good luck. I know you can do it." Then he gave me a couple of pointers. "Remember that the best operators control things, like labor and food. They're involved in their operations, engaged with their people. They stay on top of things."

"Thank you, sir. I appreciate the advice."

I walked out the door and shook my head. Events had moved quickly, and I struggled to process them all.

By the end of the day, I received one of those region-wide voicemails. "Please congratulate Ken Brown and his wife, Deidre. Ken is moving to Michigan where he'll be an owner/operator."

People came up to me. "Congratulations." Everyone seemed genuinely excited for me, even some of the people who'd once resented my fast track training program. In a strange way, I felt as if I was standing outside myself watching everything happen. It was surreal.

A week later, Deidre and I drove to Michigan to look for a rental townhouse. We still moved by faith, but everyone involved in the process had assured us the deal would be completed. Deidre and I had decided that she and the boys would stay in Chicago until the summer, and then join me in Detroit. We'd live in a rental home for a year or so, and after we got to know the area, we would look for something permanent.

As we drove through Detroit on the interstates, we got lost. I pulled off an exit on the east side to ask for directions. The area looked like the worst images I'd seen of Detroit: abandoned buildings covered in graffiti sat on every block, homeless men begged for money, and trash littered the sidewalks. I knew ghettos in Chicago, but this was a ghetto on a whole new level. We stopped at a gas station, and when I got out, I heard the door locks click behind me.

When I returned to the car with directions, Dee was crying. "I don't know if I want to live here." She pulled a tissue from her purse and blotted her tears.

I wrapped my arm around her and held her tight. "It'll be all right, baby. We'll find a nice area. I promise."

"It's more than that. My family's back in Chicago. I like Chicago."

"Just be patient. Let's see what we find on this trip before we make any decisions. It's not going to be easy to leave. I know that."

We checked into a hotel and asked the hotel manager where we could find some nice residential areas. He told us about Novi, Rochester Hills, Southfield, and West Bloomfield.

The next day we drove around. Novi and Rochester

Hills were nice, but we didn't find anything we really liked. We found a few nice places in Southfield, but still nothing that grabbed our attention. Then while driving through West Bloomfield, we stumbled across the Aldingbrook community. Manicured lawns and mature trees decorated the area.

"It's beautiful," Deidre said.

We stopped at a few rental properties and picked up some literature.

The next day, I took her on a tour of some of the potential stores. "This is for real, isn't it?" she said. With each place we visited, Deidre smiled more and more.

As we drove back to Chicago, Deidre talked about putting a deposit on one of the town homes. "This isn't going to be easy, but let's do it." She felt apprehensive, but there were no more tears.

A few days later, I'd said my good-byes to Deidre and the boys, as well as to Mu'dear and the rest of my family. My office had given me a farewell party, and I'd cleaned out my desk.

I got in the car and pulled away. I made my way onto the interstate and watched in the rearview mirror as Chicago faded into the distance. My childhood experiences made me accustomed to moving. But I'd never experienced anything like this. *I hope I'm doing the right thing. I never expected to leave my home.*

Tears filled my eyes when I thought of my family and friends—people like Mark and Archie—they were all in Chicago. Throughout my life, people who loved me had always been around. Now I was alone, and fear consumed me. *This is a mistake.* But something urged me on.

I kept driving into the unknown.

"There are three stores we'd like you to consider," John Parlow said. He took me back to three of the restaurants we'd visited on the previous trip.

I liked the one on Ten Mile Road in Southfield; it'd been rebuilt six years earlier and had a nice play area. But something bothered me about the other two. They were older restaurants and located in low volume areas. *I didn't come here to be big. I came to be successful.*

"What do you think?" John asked.

"To be honest, I only liked one of those stores."

"Well, there's one more we can look at. It's a relo."

A relo meant that the original building had been sold, and a replacement store was being built in a nearby, but better location. When we visited the relo, it was nothing but an acre of mud and a concrete slab. But a heavy flow of cars passed on the road in front. "Yes," I said. "I'm interested in this one."

"Okay, let me get together with Dee and draw up the papers. While we're waiting, is there anything I can help you with?"

I still feel over my head. I need to come up to speed real fast. "Actually, there is. I need to talk to the best owner/operator you know."

"No problem. I know just the guy."

I met with Bill Pickard in the basement office of one of his stores. He'd been an owner with McDonald's for well over twenty years. "You're a young man," he said. "How old are you?"

"Thirty-five."

"I was just a little older than you when I got started.

I'm glad they're bringing in some fresh blood." Bill spent more than an hour telling me about his business. "Do you have any questions?"

"Yes, what's it take to be successful?"

"Great question. Two things are necessary. You need to work your business—meaning you need to be very involved. And second, you need to surround yourself with good people."

I wouldn't have a problem with the first part. But I was still an organization of one. *I don't have any people.*

"By the way," Bill said. "If you need some help, I have a woman who works for me and does a great job. She handles all my administration, pays my bills, and answers my phone. I'll introduce you to her, and if she wants the work, I'll let her work with you for the first six months."

He introduced me to Caroline Jones, and she agreed to help me out. Both she and Bill were godsends. Bill had three offices in the store's basement, and Caroline worked out of one of them. "All you need to do is get yourself a file cabinet," she said.

So, Bill's office became my office. His administrative assistant became my administrative assistant. As did his accountant and tax attorney.

The next day when I arrived at the office, Caroline handed me a manila folder. "There's a fax inside that just came for you." I opened up the folder and found several sheets. Caroline had affixed sticky tabs next to the signature lines.

The cover sheet read: "You've been approved for the stores on Eight Mile Road and Ten Mile Road. Please sign and fax back these documents. Tomorrow we'll wire $3 million into your bank account for the transaction."

My mouth gaped open.

The roller coaster was screaming full speed ahead.

Here we go!

chapter twenty-nine

HELLO TO A DREAM AND GOOD-BYE TO A FRIEND

"Be slow to fall into friendship, but when thou art in, continue firm and constant." —Socrates

I t was hard to believe my entrepreneurial dreams were coming true. McDonald's gave me one month to transition the store on Ten Mile Road to my control. During that time, I worked in the store and got to know the managers and crewmembers. I wanted to get an accurate picture of how things were run, so I didn't mention I'd bought the place; they just thought I was a new supervisor. I also set up my accounting books and payroll—things I'd never done before.

At midnight, the store officially transferred to me. The next day, I had the locks changed and hosted a dinner at a Holiday Inn for all my employees. Deidre drove up from Chicago and joined us.

"I'm the new owner," I told everyone. "If you stay at this store, you'll no longer be employed by McDonald's but by the Brown Food Group. However, if you want to continue with McDonald's at another location, you're welcome to do that."

All of them stayed on with me—even the managers.

I immediately initiated changes that resulted in better-served customers and happier employees. Of course, one of the first things I changed was their uniforms. At the time, the crew wore kelly green tee shirts with Ronald McDonald on them. They were ugly. I replaced them with the uniform I'd brought to Warrenville: white oxford shirt, black tie with the golden arches on it, and black pants. They were the first uniforms of their kind in the Michigan Region.

After I took over the Ten Mile Road store, I had almost another month to prepare for the completion of the Eight Mile Road store. Several days a week, I stopped by the construction site to inspect the progress and meet with the construction manager, Eric Schwartzly. The store was the first one built under Edie's watch, so she'd been involved in its design. It included several new features, such as a larger, more efficient kitchen. But some of the items they were putting in were no different than most other McDonald's. I don't want this place to be just like the others.

One time, Eric showed me the tiles they'd picked out. They were white and plain.

"No," I said. "I'm afraid I don't like those. I want slate."

Eric's eyes widened. "You sure?"

"Yes. There's a new store in Chicago, in Bronzeville. I'll give you a phone number. Please give them a call and find out what kind they used. I want theirs."

"It'll cost you more money."

"I know. Find out how much, but do it anyway."

Then he showed me the paneling they planned to use on the bathroom walls. It's a product typically used in McDonald's and is called FRP. It's durable but looks like plastic.

"No, I don't like that, either. Let's use bathroom tiles, instead."

Eric smiled. "Okay. I like it when we do things differently."

He did a great job managing the construction. Gradually the walls and roof went up, the kitchen equipment was delivered, and the floors installed. The place came to life. When I sauntered around the construction site each night, I couldn't stop smiling.

As the opening approached, my field service consultant, David Campbell, helped me hire employees. A field service consultant is a McDonald's employee that supports owner/operators and ensures that the owners uphold the quality of the McDonald's brand. "I'll set up a trailer in the parking lot and advertise for help. We won't have any problems finding crewmembers, but finding managers may be more difficult."

He was right. We hired all the employees we needed except for the store manager. To find a manager, I contacted a city welfare-to-work program. They arranged a mini-job fair for me, and through them, I was able to fill that position.

Although my new opportunities thrilled me, sometimes the changes were overwhelming. Before, people had looked at me as just another McDonald's employee, but now I was the man in charge. My assistant, Christine, and various McDonald's people frequently gave me papers to sign; people addressed me as Mr. Brown; and about one hundred employees looked to me for their financial security. Yet, I was the youngest African-American McDonald's owner in Michigan. Everything had happened so fast.

One evening, I went home and collapsed on the sofa. I wanted to sound confident when I spoke to Deidre on the phone. She was sacrificing a lot for my dream, and she didn't need to hear me sounding wishy-washy. But alone in my townhouse, I couldn't escape the doubts. I cried.

The only person to talk to was God. "What have you done, Lord? Do you really think I'm worthy? I'm the steward of all these people."

During my childhood, Mu'dear grew closer to the Lord when she'd stayed by herself at South Bishop. We'd lost power and gas, and she sent us to stay with Granny for a few weeks. Now, my turn had come for quiet time with God. The more I prayed, the more I felt his presence.

I remembered Mu'dear's words when things looked bleak, "He didn't bring us this far to abandon us now." Her words still comforted me. He's not going to abandon me now. I just need to trust that he'll take care of things.

On June 26, I inspected the completed Eight Mile Road store. Eric lit up the large golden arches sign, and we fired up the grills and other equipment. Everything worked beautifully. It was time for the grand opening.

The next morning, we celebrated. Deidre and my boys came up, as did Mu'dear, Dad, Granny, and my sisters. Mu'dear's face beamed. I hugged each family member as they arrived. The ten of us stood together and someone snapped a family photo.

Edie and many of the people from the regional office joined us. I'd brought in balloons and entertainment for the neighborhood children. David, my field service consultant, put together a makeshift ribbon with one hundred, $1 bills. I cut the ribbon, and everyone cheered. We gave the ribbon to the local YMCA.

Throughout the day, I gave tours to everyone who stopped by. I'd filled the restaurant with live plants and piped in jazz music. The place sparkled. People tugged on me and asked to take my picture. I smiled for so many photographs that my face hurt.

And during it all, I kept hearing Mu'dear whisper in my ear, "Look at how well you've done, Kenny. Just look at you."

I'd spent part of my childhood on welfare, but now I was faring well. I was faring very well.

In retrospect, I'm grateful for the evictions and financial struggles. God, I believe, gave me those experiences to build up my endurance and teach me not to shrink from life. I learned how to deal with change and not become overwhelmed by upheaval. God knew my adult life would bring frequent changes and risk-taking, and he was preparing me for that time.

But I'm also grateful for the wisdom of my parents. Those struggles wouldn't have benefited me nearly as much if Mu'dear and Dad didn't often provide hope. They inspired me to look beyond my present situation and believe that anything was possible. Dad believed I should always stretch myself by seeking new experiences. And Mu'dear believed that God would always provide—even when I couldn't understand how. She had a faith like the woman in the Bible who believed she could be healed by touching Jesus' garment. Mu'dear trusted God's power.

I'm not the smartest guy in the world, but I've made myself available to God's purpose for my life. God has a plan for everyone, but fear prevents some people from tapping into their purpose. Like my college friend, Pete, they can't believe in the future of favor that the Lord has promised.

I've always liked King David from the Bible. He made plenty of mistakes, but he stayed close to God. God knew his heart, and David made himself available to God. The Lord knows my heart, just as he knows the hearts of all his children. If we're willing to work hard and move outside our comfort zones, we can find our heart's desires fulfilled. The Bible is full of people who God took out of comfortable situations. Abraham, Joseph, Moses, and Paul are all examples of people who God moved to fulfill his purpose.

Sometimes I wonder what my life would have been like if Mary had never fired me from Aramark. But then again, I don't think God wanted me there. Mary blessed me by letting me go, and despite the pain she caused, I'm grateful it happened. I couldn't have been successful there. And by success, I don't mean making money. Instead, I mean tapping into the current of life that flowed outside my comfort zone. By tapping into this current of life, I could serve God's purposes and lift other people up.

In looking back on my life, I see the long line of people who lifted me. They were angels sent to me for a reason, a season, or a lifetime. People like Mu'dear, Dad, Deidre, Twitch the nun, Brother Matthew who took me to Green Bay, my fraternity brothers, Jack Beard, Mark Ghee, Larry Cerf, Chuck Goldberg, and Edie Waddell. People sent to believe in me and push me to the next level.

All those angels are people of this world, and I'm indebted to them in ways I can never repay.

But I also have one angel in heaven who watches over me. I know he does.

Mark Burrell had been my steadfast friend since my first days of ninth grade. Despite his early departure from

SIU, we remained best friends through and after college. But I hadn't seen Mark for at least a year. With all my focus on proving myself at McDonald's and then the move to Michigan, I just didn't make the time. But we stayed in touch over the phone.

Some time after I opened the stores, Mark's body rejected his kidney, and he went back on dialysis. He endured a couple of surgeries, but that didn't improve things.

One day, I received a phone call from Mark's wife, Demetris. "Ken, you need to come see Mark. He's very sick." She also told me that his brother had died suddenly the day before. "Mark's in bad shape. You need to come see him as soon as you can."

I caught a plane to Chicago later that afternoon. I drove straight to Michael Reese Hospital where Mu'dear had once worked. Please, God, let him be okay.

As I walked into the hospital, I thought about how Mark always showed a strong faith in me. "Great things are going to happen to you because you have the drive and determination." Through high school and into college he'd been my biggest supporter. Where would I be without him?

I walked into his dimly lit room in the Intensive Care Unit. The room had a heavy hospital smell to it. Mark lay flat in the bed, asleep. He'd lost a lot of weight. His face was pale. IVs ran into his arms, and a machine beeped intermittently beside his bed. A photograph of his brother Chris rested on the nightstand, along with his brother's obituary.

I stood over Mark and watched him breathe. Dear Lord, please heal him.

He opened his eyes a little and saw me. "Ken Brown. Ken Brown." His voice was hoarse and slurred. "My best friend in the world. Ken Brown. How ya doing?"

"I'd be doing better if you weren't so bad off."

"Yeah, I'm not looking so good." He took a breath. "But I'll beat it. I'll be okay."

"What's going on?"

"My body's breaking down. They're running some tests. Trying to figure out what's the matter." He closed his eyes for a few seconds, and then he opened them. "They got me on some medicine..." He closed his eyes again and fell asleep.

"I'm sorry," I whispered. "I'm sorry I haven't been here for you."

I stood there and cried. Tears rolled down my face, and I didn't wipe them away. Why? Why Mark? He doesn't deserve this. He's a better man than anyone I know.

The longer I watched him—watched his labored breathing—the more I was filled with a spirit of overwhelming gratitude. Thank you, Lord, for blessing my life with this incredible man.

I leaned over, kissed him on the cheek, and walked out to talk to a nurse. "What's going on with my buddy?" I asked one of them.

"I'm sorry," she said. "We can't do anything. His insides are nearly destroyed."

I sat down in the waiting area, stunned. With all this modern technology, you can't do anything? I cried again. I could sense other visitors staring at me, but I didn't care. Why should everything be going so well with me, while Mark is losing his life? It's not right!

Mark died a few days later. My friend was gone.

I know God had sent Mark to me. The Lord knew I needed a friend, someone my age to believe in me despite the evictions and my welfare existence. When he died, Mark left a hole in my life that will be there as long as I live. But I know he's watching over me, cheering me on. And when I think about him, I'm still overcome with gratitude.

One morning while I took a shower, a memory flashed in my mind. It was that day in the high school cafeteria, sitting next to Mark and watching Jerome walk through the doors—the day my family was evicted from my home. Now look at you. This wasn't supposed to happen.

Then, like a gale-force wind, I was hit with the knowledge of God's providence—that he had blessed me in ways I could never fully understand. I had been aware of God's care before, but this time was different.

I felt the cumulative weight of God's grace and mercy, and I dropped to my knees. I covered my face with my hands. Lord, you've shown me that you're the head of my life. I'm here, at this place, because of you.

The shower washed over me like a never-ending baptism.

I don't know where you're taking me. But I surrender to you. Please use me to do your work.

Before that day, I'd thought my purpose was to run a business and serve people through food. But as I was about to learn, that was only the first step.

chapter thirty

THE TIP OF THE ICEBERG

"Success is a journey not a destination." — Ken Brown

Although I was now an owner, I still jumped in and helped my crews wherever necessary. One busy morning, I manned the drive-thru window while Miss Ruthie worked the grill behind me. She sang a hymn as we worked.

A man drove to the speaker and said, "I have two orders."

I try to be approachable with our customers and sometimes I'll joke around. "Oh, come on," I said. "Why don't you buy your buddy breakfast?"

"What?" I could hear him laughing.

"Aw, come on."

He didn't say anything.

"I tell you what," I said. "Today's your lucky day. I'll buy for both of you."

"Huh? Are you for real?"

"Yeah, I'm for real. I got you covered. Whaddya have?"

The man placed his order and drove around to the window. His face registered both shock and skepticism. "Are you sure?"

I smiled. "Sure, I'm sure. This is a glorious day. We've got to spread it around."

I'd given away food several times before. It was usually a spontaneous act—something that brings me joy. I didn't do it for recognition, and usually, no one except the customer even noticed. But this time, Miss Ruthie was watching.

Miss Ruthie was in her mid-seventies, and she reminded me of my Grandma Brown. Every morning, Miss Ruthie came to the restaurant at five o'clock and cooked the eggs and bacon. She sang hymns whenever she worked. After a few hours, she'd take a break, grab her purse, and go sit in the back. There, she read her morning devotions.

"You know, I go to church every Sunday and Wednesday," she said after I gave away the free breakfasts. "But, I believe it's often better to see God's Word than it is to hear it."

She turned the bacon over. "What you just did for that customer, that helps me see the Word."

"Thank you, Miss Ruthie."

She glanced at me. "Been watching you, Mr. Brown. You really care about people. I think God is going to use you as a messenger."

Ever since the morning I fell to my knees in the shower, I believed God had something else in store for me. "McDonald's is just the tip of the iceberg," a voice inside me seemed to say.

God had changed me. I'd always tried to serve my customers with excellence. But during the first two years as an owner, I began to see my purpose in life as more than food. *I can use my background and personality to encourage people.*

I dove into a deeper relationship with Jesus Christ. Deidre saw the difference in me. I expressed my faith more openly and fervently—just like Mu'dear had done. I became more involved in my church and read the Bible almost every day. I hosted small group meetings—which we called Word Cell meetings—at one of my stores. There, we studied and discussed the Word. My understanding of God's providence humbled me and motivated me to share it with others.

One morning as I drove to work, I listened to Tavis Smiley talk on the radio. Mr. Smiley is a popular African-American radio and television personality who has contributed to programs such as NPR and PBS. On the program that morning, he shared how he'd experienced some recent troubles, and how people had written letters to lift him up and inspire him. In honor of those people, he announced, he would publish a compilation book with one hundred, true and inspiring short stories. He would call the book *Keeping the Faith: Stories of Love, Courage, Healing and Hope from Black America.*

Mu'dear use to say I should write a book about my life. "You certainly had enough drama." *Maybe I should try to write something for this book.* I pulled the car over and wrote down the address for story submissions.

That night, I couldn't sleep. I kept thinking about writing my story. Finally, I got out of bed and went to my office. I stayed up most of the night writing, and the words flowed out as I scribbled away. It had to be less than 1,000 words, so I spent a lot of the time trying to remove stuff.

In the morning, I showed it to Deidre. She gave me that sly smile she shows whenever I get a wild idea. Then she read it. "This could work." She tweaked a few things, corrected some spelling, and handed it back to me. "Send it in," she said. "See what happens."

A few months later, I received an envelope in the mail. In the upper left corner it read, "Tavis Smiley Talks."

No way. I tore it open and yanked out the letter.

"Congratulations," it said. "Your story has been selected to be in my latest book."

"Yes!" I ran upstairs and showed the letter to Deidre, and then I called Mu'dear.

The publication of my story motivated me even more to share words of encouragement. Words have power—either positive or negative—and something is activated when words are spoken or written down for others. When God made the earth, he spoke it into creation. "Let there be light," he said.

After the Tavis Smiley book came out, I gave away many copies. One copy I gave to Pam Perry, a public relations representative with Hermanoff and Associates. She did PR work on behalf of my stores and other McDonald's in the area.

"Your story was great," she said later. "You should consider turning it into a book of your own."

"You know, my mother use to say our story would make a good book."

"It would, Ken. Your life is a ministry. The way you do business is different. You interact with people and serve them the way a minister would."

Me? A minister? I'd never thought about it quite like that.

But that night, I looked up the word "minister" in the

dictionary. It had many different meanings, but originally it meant "servant." *Maybe that's why I've always been drawn to the service industry. I'm built to serve.*

Pam helped me get into public speaking by arranging for me to speak at some local schools. I had a great time talking to children and encouraging them not to let the challenges of life get them down. I put a lot of energy into my talks, and I tried to leave them thinking they could accomplish anything.

"You're a great speaker," a teacher told me.

"Yeah, I could open for Les Brown," I said jokingly.

Les Brown was one of the top African-American motivational speakers in the world. I'd watched several of his videos when I worked at Kraft and always remembered his encouragement to believe in myself.

Later, Pam gave me a book written by Jerome Edmonson, the first black franchise owner of a Denny's restaurant. The book was titled: *Maximizing Misfortune.* "You should read this. You two have a lot in common." Mr. Edmonson was also from Detroit.

It was a short book, and that night I read the entire thing. I couldn't put it down. We had similar backgrounds, and I could see how the Lord had carried him just like he'd carried me. I felt the urge to contact him, but I didn't act right away.

A week later, I glanced at the book sitting on my nightstand and noticed Mr. Edmonson's contact information. It said he was now president of the Christian Business Network, located at Nine Mile Road and Evergreen, in

Southfield, Michigan.

No way! Both of my restaurants were in Southfield, one on Eight Mile Road and one on Ten Mile Road; his office was right between the two. *Here we go again.*

The next morning, I got in my car to drive to work. Except I didn't go to work. Instead, I drove to the intersection of Nine Mile and Evergreen to see if I could find the offices of the Christian Business Network. I finally found the small office building and went inside. In the waiting area a glass case displayed Jerome Edmonson's book, as well as some audiotapes by Myles Munroe and Bishop Eddie Long—two famous African-American pastors and motivational speakers. Mu'dear was a big fan of Eddie Long.

A woman came out to the reception area and greeted me. I pointed to the book in the display case. "That book is why I'm here. My name's Ken Brown, and I own a couple of McDonald's down the street."

"You own the McDonald's on Eight Mile? That's a great place. I go there all the time."

"Thank you, ma'am."

"Your people are so kind, and it's the cleanest McDonald's I've ever seen."

I thanked her again, but I really didn't want to talk about McDonald's. "I'd like to meet Mr. Edmonson if possible. We have some things in common, and I want to learn more about the Christian Business Network."

"Well, he's not here right now, but I'll be sure to pass along the message."

I handed her my card, and she gave me some literature about CBN. She explained it was a network of Christian business leaders, or kingdom business leaders as she put it, that gather for fellowship and sharing ideas on how to be servants to their customers and companies.

"I see myself as a servant leader, also, and I'd like to be involved in what he's doing."

I got back in the car and before I even arrived at my store, the cell phone rang.

"Ken Brown?" the voice said. "This is Jerome Edmonson of CBN. Ms. Johnson was so excited after meeting you that she insisted I call you right away."

We scheduled a half-hour meeting for that Friday.

I met Jerome in the conference room of his office, and we hit it off immediately. Our half-hour meeting ran more than two hours. We talked about our backgrounds and how to use our gifts to build up others. At the end of our meeting, he said, "I have a CBN conference coming up, and if you're interested, I'd like you to speak."

"I'd be glad to." I figured it'd be a small gathering. I'd spoken at the schools, so that would be another step up.

"Great. As soon as you have a chance, please e-mail a photograph of yourself for the brochure."

A few weeks later, a sample brochure arrived at work. It was a large, tri-fold glossy, and on the front it read: *Christian Business Network Conference: Maximizing Wealth and Resources.* I opened it and saw the photographs of the presenters. At the top were pictures of Myles Munroe and Eddie Long! And near the bottom was a picture of Kenneth Brown.

What have I gotten myself into now? I was on the same page with two of the most famous pastors in America. I took the brochure inside and showed it to Miss Ruthie.

"See," she said. "I told you God had something in mind for you."

Then I called Mu'dear and told her I would be sharing the stage with Eddie Long.

"Oh, my! *The* Eddie Long? Well look what the Lord's gone and done now."

As the date for the conference approached, I grew nervous. Miss Ruthie offered some advice. "If you stay focused on God, he'll carry you through. Before you go on stage, try saying this prayer, 'Lord, speak to me, through me, and for me. Let your Word be rightly told. Let me be decreased so you will be increased.'"

I wrote down the prayer and put it in my pocket.

On the day of the conference, I drove to the Ritz-Carlton Hotel in Dearborn. My stomach churned. *I hope I'm up to this.* I walked into the ballroom and stepped back when I saw the crowd—five hundred strong. Mu'dear and her lifelong friend Claudette were also there.

When I went up to give them hugs, Claudette cried. "My, my, my, Kenny. I'm so proud of you."

I visited with them for awhile and then went backstage. I listened to Eddie Long speak and then to Myles Munroe. I knew the audience was there to see them and not necessarily me. While Mr. Munroe spoke, my knees started feeling wobbly, and sweat beaded on my forehead. *Why me, Lord? I can understand everything up to this point, but why this?*

Almost immediately a word popped into my head: providence. It was part of his plan, and he was using me—just like I'd asked him to that time in the shower. I took out Miss Ruthie's prayer and repeated it several times.

I felt at peace. *I'm supposed to be here.*

As I stepped up on the stage, God took over. I felt as comfortable as if I'd been hanging out with friends at Willibrord Catholic High School. I made people laugh and even saw a few tears. I introduced my mother while I was on stage. "Mu'dear, remember you promised me as far as my eye could see? Well, look at this. Isn't this awesome! We're at the Ritz-Carlton. Can you believe it? They've got marble floors, Mu'dear, and real towels in the bathroom."

I talked to the audience about my life, taking risks, and tapping into God's plan. "If we do our part, if we strive for excellence, then God will use our gifts to make this a better world."

When I finished, the crowd gave me a standing ovation. I looked at Mu'dear. Now she was crying along with Claudette.

After the conference wrapped up, the cameraman, Derek, approached me. He had filmed all the speakers. "Wow, man, that was powerful," he said. "I can get you some DVDs of your speech if you'd like."

A week later, Derek brought a box of DVDs to me at the store. "The more I see your speech," he said, "the more I see how powerful the message is. It's powerful on many levels, not just the McDonald's thing. You should take your message on the road."

"I'd like to." I said. Then I chuckled. "Now all I need to do is open for Les Brown."

"Les Brown?"

"Sure, why not?"

With that, Derek reached into his bag and pulled out his cell phone. He dialed a number and waited. I could hear a voice on the other. "It's his voicemail," Derek said.

"Whose voicemail?"

He spoke into the phone. "Hi, Les. This is Derek in Michigan. I've met this guy named Ken Brown, and I think you need to meet him. He's got a great story. He'd be great for the network."

Yeah, right. This guy's messing with me. I don't have time for this.

I stood up and shook his hand. "How much do I owe you for the DVDs?" I paid him, and he left.

A few weeks later, Derek stopped back by the store. "How were the DVDs?"

"They were great."

"Did Les ever call you?"

You're really going to milk this, aren't you? "Nope. No call," I said and sighed impatiently.

He picked up his phone again and dialed a number.

"Hello, Les. This is Derek. That guy I was telling you about, Ken Brown, he's right here." Derek handed me the phone.

I looked at Derek. *Huh?*

"Go ahead," he said. "He wants to talk to you."

"Is this for real?"

I put the phone to my ear and cleared my throat. "Uh, Mr. Brown? This is Ken Brown."

"My cousin?" the man on the phone said, chuckling. "How you doing? Derek's told me great things about you."

No way.

"How can I help you?" he asked.

"Um, I've always admired your work, sir." Then I proceeded to tell him the short version of my story. "Is this something I should speak about?"

"It's got real potential. I'd love to hear more," he said. "I tell you what. I'm giving a seminar in Orlando in a couple of weeks. I'm meeting with some other aspiring speakers during that time. Can you meet me there so we can talk some more?"

"I'll be there, sir. Absolutely."

I hung up the phone and handed it slowly back to